be
Confident
be
YOU :)

Published by Collins
An imprint of HarperCollins Publishers
Westerhill Road, Bishopbriggs,
Glasgow G64 2QT

HarperCollins Publishers
Macken House,
39/40 Mayor Street Upper,
Dublin 1
D01 C9W8
Ireland

www.harpercollins.co.uk

978-0-00-854520-8

Printed in Italy

10 9 8 7 6 5 4 3 2 1

Thanks to all the team at HarperCollins
for championing confidence, and special
thanks to Michelle I'Anson and Lauren
Murray for all their wonderful support,
hard work and enthusiasm for **Be Confident
Be You.** Thank you Josephine Dellow for the
magical illustrations.

This book is dedicated to my own teens,
Frankie and Annalise, who I love with all
my heart. May you both always have the
confidence to follow your own path. It is
also dedicated to Naomi C who I admire
hugely and believe is simply fabulous.
Shine your lovely light, Naomi! And to
Helen and Na, whose confidence in me and
my dreams has supported me more times
than I can possibly count. I am forever
grateful. Love you both so very much.

#beconfidentbeyou

be Confident be you :)

THE TEENAGE GUIDE

Becky Goddard-Hill

illustrated by Josephine Dellow

what is confidence?

Confidence is having trust in yourself and your abilities. It is believing you can cope and that you will be okay (even in hard times). It is knowing that you can rely on yourself.

Your teen years bring new challenges and opportunities, plus an expectation that you will approach them more independently. Feeling capable and confident will help you to make the most of this time, and to gain experience, knowledge and skills that you can take into adulthood.

are you born confident?

Some people make being confident look easy, and you may think they were just born that way. But as well as genetics, there are many things that affect confidence:

- You may have grown up with praise, encouragement and support so you feel valued and have high self-esteem.

- You may have had opportunities to challenge yourself so you feel capable and competent.

- You may have been encouraged to be independent and solve problems and this may have led to self-reliance and self-trust.

Alternately you may have been bullied, struggled with friendships or found school tricky, and as a result your confidence may be low.

Upbringing, opportunities and life events can all impact how your confidence develops. But confidence isn't fixed and it is entirely possible to rewire your brain in a way that enables you to feel confident and capable of taking action in line with that.

the teen years and your brain

Your brain rewires and reorganises itself in your teens and this can feel overwhelming and confusing. You will sometimes feel emotional and exhausted due to these changes. The changes happening in your brain, combined with the stress of teen life, can make these years feel tough.

But don't worry. You can build the confidence you need to help you cope with the situations and stressors you encounter, in order to trust in yourself to make good decisions.

what is in the book?

The aim of this book is to show you many of the ways you can boost your confidence.

It is split into three sections:

Each of these sections looks at issues you might face in your teen years and areas you might wish to improve or strengthen in order to make your life easier, more positive and more productive. Science underpins each of the issues covered so you know why, as well as how, the advice works.

Most of the topics have an activity too so you can have a go at putting your learning into practice.

how to use this book

This book is yours to read entirely as you wish. You could go straight to the topics that interest you or are currently relevant to you, or you could read it in page order. Some of the topics may not have impacted you yet or they may cover issues you are already comfortable dealing with.

Do try and have a go at all the activities though, as nothing helps you learn or grow your confidence quite as much as experience.

you will need...

/ a notebook – for some of the activities in which you need to write, draw or make lists

● an open mind – some of these ideas may sound a little quirky but try them out, they might surprise you

● someone you can talk to about what you read, to explore the ideas more (but it's fine too if your confidence journey is yours alone).

Confidence strategies are simple to learn and yet super powerful. Time spent absorbing these will benefit you throughout your life. You absolutely can become more confident whilst still being entirely yourself.

confident thoughts

:)

it starts with you

The only two things you have the power to control in life are your thoughts and your actions, but this is great news because these both have a huge impact on how your life turns out.

Thoughts affect how you feel, and how you feel affects how you behave – so thoughts are important and powerful.

you get to choose

You might not realise this yet, but you are absolutely the one who can choose your thoughts and change them if they are not helping you.

Self-doubt, fear, blame and worry can lead you to feel unconfident and helpless, and these feelings can lead to inaction and avoidance.

It's important that your thoughts are helpful and that they support you in feeling capable and confident. By improving your confidence by taking control of your thoughts, you will be able to go for your goals and take on any challenges.

Being able to manage your thoughts takes some practice because, during your teens, your brain has a tendency to be both negative and emotionally driven. But time spent practising confident thinking is worth it because your thoughts affect everything.

Let's take a look at what you can do to think in a way that will benefit you and boost your confidence.

1 me, myself and I

Accept no one's definition of your life, but define yourself.
Harvey Fierstein, actor and writer

Liking and accepting who you are can have a huge impact on your self-confidence.

Society, friends and family will put labels on you, defining you by your age, appearance, skin colour, culture, faith, abilities, gender and sexuality. They will also give you labels according to their opinion of your personality, such as silly, hard-working or unmotivated.

There is not much you can do about how others define you (unless they are offensive, in which case it is important to make a stand).

What matters is that you are comfortable with, proud of, and accepting of your own identity.

questioning who you are

In your teens you may start to question (and reject) things that made up your identity when you were a child.

This can feel confusing as what you know about yourself may begin to feel shaky and uncertain. But don't worry – according to science this is totally normal.

the science bit

The psychologist Erik Erikson called this tricky period, when teenagers work through their sense of who they are, *Identity versus role confusion*. According to Erikson, it is vital to explore identity at this age so that the path you take in adulthood is one that you have chosen yourself rather than one that has been chosen for you.

identity is not set

At the age of 10 you might have been known for being an elite swimmer; aged 15 you might not swim at all. At 18 you might start to compete again, having missed being in the pool.

At 12 you may have had your first boyfriend, at 16 you may decide you possibly prefer girls and at 18 you might be sure you only like girls or have gone back to liking boys, or both, and that's okay too.

Identity is fluid, you never have to put labels on yourself (unless you want to), no matter what age you are.

Exploring your identity can be daunting, especially if it goes against other people's expectations.

But (and this is important) you are the one person you will spend your whole life with, so what matters most is that you don't disappoint yourself.

changes

You might work out who you are by experimenting with different appearances or interests.

You might join a new club, read up on different perspectives or see the school counsellor to chat things over.

Changes that you make may completely baffle your parents, who will be left wondering where 'you' have gone. You may need to explain to them it's a normal part of your development and that you would like to have their support.

what helps?

In order to confidently explore your identity, it can help to:

1 find role models for the things you care about

2 think about what sparks you and makes you feel alive

3 explore your values and the things that you like best about yourself

4 meet like-minded people.

Figuring out who you want to be is time well spent.

who are you?

If you were to describe yourself to someone else (without any attempt to please anyone or sound cool) what ten words might you use?

Freedom to be who you are may be challenging but your identity is a precious thing and owning it and delighting in it will bring you confidence.

be confident be you...

...by being your true self.

2 faulty thinking

Change your thoughts and you change your world.
Norman Vincent Peale, author

There is so much going on in your teen years, it can feel overwhelming. And when you are overwhelmed, it can be hard to think straight.

But things are rarely as bad as you might first think, and questioning your thoughts can really help.

Imagine you have forgotten your English homework and your lesson is coming up straight after lunch. You are upset; you spent ages on it and your teacher is strict.

It is normal to feel annoyed or upset with yourself when you make a mistake. But there are some types of *faulty thinking* that can make situations like these seem worse than they are.

Let's take a look at how faulty thinking might work in this situation, and how you can fix it.

fixing faulty thinking

catastrophising

Catastrophising is when your mind leaps to the worst-case scenario. So, having forgotten your homework you spend lunchtime in tears and consider missing class because it's GOING TO BE AWFUL and you will be in MASSIVE TROUBLE.

Fix this thought!

Rate your problem on a scale of 0 to 10, where 0 is no problem and 10 is a disaster. How big is forgetting your homework really? It's probably not above a 5 and doesn't require a dramatic response. Remind yourself it's natural to forget things or make mistakes sometimes.

mind-reading

You sit through lunch worrying about how your teacher is now going to think you are a liar, stupid or lazy.

Fix this thought!

You never know what someone else will think so don't assume you can mind-read. It is entirely possible that your teacher left something they needed at home today too and will understand. Simply wait and see how they respond.

all-or-nothing thinking

You spend your break moaning to your friend that your whole day is now ruined.

Fix this thought!

Don't write off a whole day because of one mistake, instead look for some balance. Didn't you score a basket at PE this morning? Tell your friend about the good stuff too and get a better sense of perspective.

overgeneralising or labelling

You are so cross about leaving your homework behind, you tell yourself you are always messing up and have a terrible memory. You are overgeneralising – making a sweeping statement based on just one incident.

Fix this thought!

Remind yourself that in 3 years of English lessons you've never forgotten your homework before so it isn't the case that you have a bad memory or always mess up.

blaming

You tell yourself it's your mum's fault you didn't pack your homework because she got you up late. It can be easier to blame other people, but is it fair?

Fix that thought!

Take responsibility for not packing your homework and commit to doing it the night before in future.

Once you start to see how faulty thoughts make everything worse you can start to challenge them. Thinking logically, rather than just emotionally, helps minimise how awful a situation seems and helps you handle life more confidently and with a clearer mind.

be confident be you...

...by recognising and fixing faulty thinking.

3 the comparison trap

> Comparison with myself brings improvement. comparison with others brings discontent.
> Betty Jamie Chung, author

Who do you compare yourself to?

Is it the smart guy you sit next to in Maths? Is it your super-sporty sister? Perhaps it's an influencer you follow who just seems to have it all going on?

social comparison theory

Social comparison theory was developed back in 1954 by psychologist Leon Festinger. He found it was instinctive for people to judge themselves in relation to other people and use them as a benchmark to measure their own skills and performance.

He also discovered that whilst it was natural for people to do this it, was not always helpful.

the problem with social comparison

Upward social comparison is when you see others doing 'better than you'. It can motivate you and inspire you to try harder or it can seriously knock your confidence if you consider that you fall short.

Downward social comparison is when you compare yourself to someone who seems 'worse off' than you. This can make you feel good about your achievements but can also stop you feeling you need to progress.

Comparing yourself to others has its pros and cons, affecting both confidence and motivation in good and bad ways. It's important to be aware of any negative feelings that arise out of comparing yourself to others, so they don't interfere with your self-belief or make you jealous, frustrated or unhappy.

things aren't always what they seem

Everyone's journey through life contains highs and lows. Your sporty sister may envy your skill as a scientist, the stunning influencer will (almost definitely) be showing filtered highlights from their life, and the maths genius may have a tricky homelife.

No one has it all easy or shows you the whole picture, so comparisons that you make with others will always be inaccurate and incomplete.

triggers

If an account you follow on social media makes you feel inadequate, unfollow, and replace it with one that makes you laugh or think. You have the power to make yourself happier, and what you look at hugely impacts that.

If you have a friend who triggers your insecurities because they boast or put you down, notice how it makes you feel and move on.

Being aware of, and avoiding, triggers that knock your confidence is powerful self-care.

who should you compete with?

The best person you can ever compete with in life is yourself.

Forget focusing on where you stand relative to others, it's time to focus on how you can improve in relation to yourself. This is a great way to boost confidence.

be your best self

Have a think about what you did yesterday that was kind. Next, consider how you could better that today, by being even kinder.

Put that kindness into action and you will feel just great about yourself.

You can always improve – but you only need to compete with yourself.

be confident be you...

...by avoiding the comparison trap.

4 calm and in control

Nothing can bring you peace
but yourself.
Ralph Waldo Emerson, preacher and poet

It's hard to feel confident when you are worried, because
your mind is focused on things that might go, or have gone,
wrong.

Everyone worries sometimes – it's normal and a sign that
you care. But sometimes worries can cloud and crowd
minds, affect behaviour and cause physical discomfort,
which is why it's important to manage them well.

By learning these simple strategies to calm your body and
mind, you will manage your worries with more confidence.

mindfulness

Mindfulness is concentrating on what's happening right
here, right now, not in the past or future (which is where
worry lives). This gives your brain a break and helps to clear
your head.

Mindfulness activities include colouring mandalas, yoga, baking, dancing, crafting, gardening or even cloud-watching. Try them all to find your favourite.

The key to making experiences mindful is to engage your senses. If you are cloud-watching, smell the grass, focus on the cloud shapes, feel the breeze and sense your body relax. This will put you entirely 'in the moment'.

With a clearer mind you will be able to address your worries more rationally.

control circles

 Control circles can also help. Simply draw three circles (as on the next page) and fill them with your worries, putting them in the right areas according to how much control of them you have.

If you put energy into concerns that are out of your control, you will feel helpless. Let them go. Put time and energy into the areas you can control (your thoughts and actions) to feel more positive, empowered and confident.

You could also try writing worries down or talking them over. You could set aside some 'worry time' so they aren't on your mind all the time, or you could use positive affirmations such as 'I am calm and in control'.

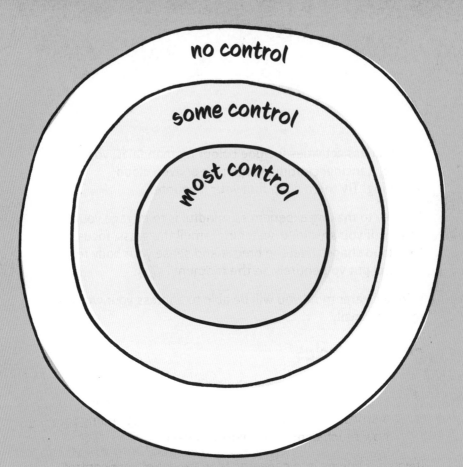

no control

some control

most control

breathing deeply

A tense, anxious mind creates a tense, anxious body, but when you calm one down the other calms down too.

Anxiety makes your breath shallow and irregular, and this makes you feel stressed. But when you breathe deeply, more air flows into your body and your heartbeat steadies, telling your brain all is calm and well.

Scientists at Stanford University, discovered that brains contain 175 brain cells that focus on breath and alter your state of mind depending on what your breath is doing. Changing your breathing is powerful.

Try belly breathing:

- place both hands on your tummy, fingers touching
- inhale deeply through your nose
- as your tummy inflates, your fingers will separate
- breathe out slowly through pursed lips
- your fingers will rejoin as your tummy flattens
- repeat until you feel calm.

Other ways to calm your body include walking, warm baths, yoga, tai-chi and meditation. Never underestimate how much calming a body calms a worried mind.

The fear-busting and problem-solving sections of this book will help you face your worries, but work on being calm first and you will find it much easier.

walk away from your worries

Take a walk in nature, with no distractions. Engage your senses and focus on what you can see, hear, smell and touch. Let your busy mind completely relax.

be confident be you...

...by being calm and in control.

5 fear of failure

Giving up is the only sure way to fail.
Gena Showalter, author

From social media to school, the pressures to achieve can be intense in your teens and you might well feel overwhelmed.

If fear of failing holds you back, then you could miss out on some of the best opportunities life may bring. As the saying goes, 'You miss every shot you don't take', so you need to gather your courage and get in the game.

the science bit

Extreme fear of failing is called *atychiphobia* and psychologists have found it causes feelings of anxiety. These fears largely stem from feelings of shame and embarrassment around failure and worries about disappointing others. This can cause people to avoid situations where they could fail, in order to reduce their anxiety.

But giving in to such fears does not make for an exciting life and nor does it build confidence.

enjoy the journey

The trick is to associate success with the effort and energy you put into a project, not simply the outcome. Take pride in giving things a go and enjoy the journey rather than pinning everything on the final destination.

don't wait to feel confident

You don't wait to feel awake before you roll out of bed, you just get up because you know there are things you have to do. Take the same approach with opportunities – just give them a go, don't wait till you feel confident. Confidence comes when you act.

live with uncertainty

Sometimes you have to make a choice in the face of possible failure. You might apply for a competitive job or try out for drama school and the odds might be against you, but your only other option is to not try at all. Accept the uncertainty – the payoff could be amazing.

help yourself

If you are tempted to not do something through fear of failing, try helping yourself instead. Ask for support, find the tools you need and work on creative problem-solving. Action vanquishes fear.

know you can cope

At some point along the way, you will fail, it is inevitable. Of course you will feel disappointed, but be kind and compassionate to yourself, lean in to your support network and you will be okay. Failing is part of being human. You will survive. Look at when you have bounced back before. Focus on how you did that and draw on those skills again.

view failure differently

Try and see failure as an opportunity to learn, a launch pad to trying something new, an experiment that didn't quite work. It is temporary. Face it with curiosity, explore why you failed and make a plan to try again or to try something else.

Failure is not a stop sign; it is a signpost to your next step.

famous failures

Search 'famous failures' and you will see how failing to reach a goal can actually inspire and motivate people.

Michael Jordan, one of the best basketball players of all time, didn't even make it into his high school basketball team. This spurred him on.

Walt Disney was once fired from a job at a newspaper by an editor who said he 'lacked imagination and had no good ideas'. Walt never gave up!

Who are your favourite 'failed-a-few-times' heroes?

be confident be you...

...by facing your fear of failure head-on.

6 know your strengths

Always remember, you have within you the strength, the patience and the passion to reach for the stars to change the world.

Harriet Tubman, social activist

No matter how uncomfortable it might feel there are huge benefits to knowing your strengths and giving them your time and attention.

If you focus on the things that make you feel weak and inferior, then you will increasingly notice things in your life that support you to feel that way. Consequently, you will feel weaker.

If you focus on the things that make you feel strong and confident you will become increasingly aware of times you act with strength and of the chances you have to do so. As a result, you will feel stronger.

Thoughts are powerful.

the science bit

It is scientifically proven that what you focus on gets bigger. It's all thanks to the *reticular activating system* (RAS), a bundle of nerves that sit in the brainstem.

The RAS works as a filter. It looks at the vast amount of data available from every sensory thing happening in your world, then presents the pieces it considers important into your conscious awareness. Therefore, what you focus on and think about matters.

It's the reason why, if you are wearing a yellow top, you'll see loads of people wearing one too and why, if you are in a noisy room and someone says your name, you will immediately hear it.

Some people call receiving more of what you think about, the law of attraction, but actually it's just your super-clever brain filter at work seeking out and letting in what it knows you are focused on.

So, focus on your strengths if you want to feel stronger and you will see more opportunities to use them and more evidence of them in action. You will also find your self-esteem and self-confidence rise because of this focus.

do you know your strengths?

Take a look at the strengths below and think about which ones you possess.

Give the *absolutely yes* ones 3 ticks, the *yes* ones 2 ticks, the *sometimes* ones 1 tick and leave blank the ones you haven't developed YET. If you find it difficult to recognise your strengths, think about how other people might describe you in these terms.

Honesty	Empathy
Gentleness	Generosity
Trustworthiness	Energy
Artistic skills	Curiosity
Good memory	Leadership
Resourcefulness	Self-control
Organisation	Motivation
Loyalty	Adventurousness
Assertiveness	Courage
Thoughtfulness	Flexibility
Intelligence	Optimism
Wisdom	Caring
Patience	Helpfulness
Kindness	Bravery
Sense of fun	Confidence
Liveliness	Friendliness
Consideration	Determination
Sensitivity	Resilience

saving the day

Imagine you are stranded on a desert island with twenty 7-year-olds. There are tears and tantrums, and all the kids are just desperate to get home. It is clear that it is your job to take charge.

You are allowed to use six of your strengths to get you all safely home – which ones would you use and why?

You can either write this up as a story or talk it over with someone.

How fabulous that you already have all the strengths and skills you need to save twenty stranded 7-year-olds! You have every right to feel confident.

be confident be you...

...by knowing, valuing and focusing on your many strengths.

35

7 negativity

Dwelling on the negative simply contributes to its power.
Shirley MacLaine, actress

Do you look at what's wrong more than what's right? Dwell on a criticism longer than a compliment? If you do, it's not because you have a 'bad attitude', it's because your brain is hardwired to do so.

the science bit

Our tendency to pay more attention to bad things than good is believed by scientists to be a result of evolution. In ancient times being aware of bad, dangerous things quite literally kept us alive.

Humans have, of course, evolved since then but studies show brains remain more instinctively responsive to negatives than positives due to what's called *negativity bias*.

Because of *neuroplasticity* (the ability our brains have to rewire and grow), focusing on the positives will, over time, cause new neural pathways to be built and make thinking positively more of a habit. You just have to put in the work.

look for the good stuff

When things go wrong it is natural to feel upset, it would be unhealthy to try to deny that. But *only* focusing on what's wrong isn't healthy either.

If you go to a party and the person you fancy ignores you all evening you could choose to see the evening as ruined. Or you could say, 'Well that bit was rubbish but the music was fantastic and I had a laugh with my friends.'

By looking at the whole picture you will see that whilst life is not perfect, it is often great. This knowledge will keep your spirits and your confidence up.

You don't need to wait for things to change in order to feel good, you just need to change how you look at things.

extra attention

It takes more for positive experiences to be remembered than negative, so you need to give them extra attention.

Tell people your good news, make scrapbooks, take photos, bullet journal the lovely stuff and give it the focus it deserves.

the little ink splat story

One morning a teacher handed out test papers to her students as a 'surprise'. Their test was a blank sheet with a small ink splat on it.

'Just write about what you see,' said the teacher. Her confused students set to work.

When the teacher read the papers, she was unsurprised to see that each student wrote about the ink splat and why it was 'spoiling the paper'.

None of them wrote about all the blank space around the splat and it's potential. They simply focused on the tiny splat.

The teacher explained to the students that people tended to do this in life too, focusing on something tiny that 'spoils' things despite all the unspoilt things being so much bigger. She explained what a waste that was of all the good stuff.

Can you think of an ink splat you paid way too much attention to this week?

Keep your eyes peeled for ink splats and don't forget to look at the whole page.

be confident be you...

...by reducing the power of negativity and focusing more on the positives.

8 building on your success

> ## Self-confidence is the memory of success.
> ### David Storey, writer

When times are tough or things go wrong it can be tempting to consider your life to be a disaster and yourself a hopeless non-achiever. Intense feelings happen a lot in the teen years because the emotional part of your brain is super sensitive and your thinking brain doesn't always keep up.

But just because you FEEL something doesn't mean it's true.

If you believe you don't have what it takes to try things right now, it is time to pause, take stock and insist your thinking brain does some work.

you are astonishing

When you intentionally search back over your lifetime for the things you have achieved and are proud of, you will see that you are in fact incredible and made up of tough stuff.

Knowing this about yourself is important and useful. It helps you appreciate that you are strong and skilful and that you can do (and have done) difficult things.

It's easy to be unconfident if you believe you haven't achieved anything. But that's certainly not the case. You have achieved so many things since you were a baby and you have a right to be confident. The evidence is right there in your memory bank.

the science bit

Participants in a nostalgia-based study, who were encouraged to look back at their past successes and happier times, reported feeling more optimistic about the future and better about themselves. During rough times, reflecting on happier, more positive memories reminded them that life can be good and that they were capable.

Looking back at the good stuff can propel you forwards with confidence.

timeline of achievements

Draw a horizontal line across the middle of a sheet of
A4 paper in landscape. Now split your line into equal parts
according to how many years you have been alive. This is
your timeline. Next, draw lines off your timeline so you can
add the things you have achieved or are proud of.

You might have to ask an older member of your family
for some of the dates of your earliest achievements. You
could include things like:

- learning to walk

- swimming 10 metres

- being able to ride a bike

- making your first friend

- coping with moving house or school

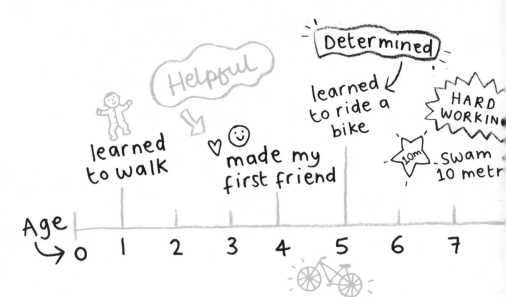

- going on an overnight school trip

- travelling to school by yourself

- your first date.

Once you have your list, think about what qualities you had that enabled you to achieve all these things. Try to come up with ten of these and write them round the edge of your timeline paper. Were you hard-working, brave, determined? Did you have good balance or a good memory, were you friendly? What was it about you that made this stuff possible?

When you are having a wobble, looking back at your timeline will give your confidence a great boost.

be confident be you...

...by recognising all you have achieved and taking confidence from that.

9 good enough is good enough

Waiting for perfect is never as smart as making progress.
Seth Godin, businessman and author

If your confidence rests on perfect end results, then you probably won't feel confident all that often. Life is rarely perfect.

No matter how hard you try, the sleekest hairstyle can be frizzed by the rain and your dog really might eat your homework.

If you can cope when things go wrong, then perfectionism probably isn't a problem for you. But, if you strive for success at the expense of your health, fall apart when you make a mistake and are highly critical of yourself or others, then perfectionism may be an issue.

the problem with perfectionism

Psychologists have found that perfectionists are often anxious, easily frustrated, unconfident and struggle with low mood. Feeling this way takes its toll and perfectionism has been linked to serious mental health problems such as eating disorders and depression.

Perfectionism can also cause people to procrastinate, avoiding what they need to do through fear it won't work out. Alternately they might spend hours trying to get a tiny thing just right and this can be exhausting and frustrating.

Let's take a look at perfectionism in action.

a tale of two artists

Jo and Jai are in art class. Jo rips up drawing after drawing because he can't get it right. The class ends and Jo has nothing to show for his efforts, except his frustration. Jai has been experimenting with colours and shapes. He has rough results but feels he learned a lot and he's excited about the next session.

Who do you think is feeling more confident about their art?

Aiming for progress, not perfection, boosts both confidence and HAPPINESS levels.

what helps?

Successful outcomes are hit and miss but there are some things you can always control:

Effort – You can always choose whether you show up, are enthusiastic and see something through. Effort goes a long way towards achievement and makes the process more fun. A good effort will make you proud of yourself no matter what the end result.

Response – You can see a low Maths grade as an opportunity to ask for help or as a sign you are stupid. How you respond to imperfect results makes all the difference and is always a choice.

Positive self-talk – According to Gordon Flett, a leading researcher on perfectionism, perfectionists tend to talk to themselves badly. If you catch yourself doing this, stop! Treat yourself to words of encouragement, kindness and motivation instead.

perfectly imperfect

Have a think about what you would say in the following scenarios:

Your best friend tells you she is giving up her beloved running because she has lost her last three races.

You mum has spent 5 hours trying to write the perfect email to your school, complaining about homework levels, and is about to admit defeat.

I imagine you have been supportive in your responses, encouraging those you care about to let go of perfectionism but not give up.

Try treating yourself with the same compassion and support when perfectionism threatens your confidence.

Good enough is good enough, and being successful is never more important than being happy and well.

be confident be you...

...by striving for progress not perfection and treating yourself with kindness.

10 future plans

Tell me, what is it you plan to do with your one wild and precious life?

Mary Oliver, poet

What do you plan to do when you leave school?

Have you considered post-16 life and whether you are going to study, prepare for uni, do a vocational course or perhaps an apprenticeship?

Are you filled with confidence about your future or does the thought terrify you?

plans change (and so do you)

Plans for the future need not be fixed; you can always change your mind about what you want to do.

You might find you aren't even suited to what you once considered your dream job.

When I was 16, I believed that I wanted to be a spy. When I told the recruitment interviewer this, she asked how many people I'd discussed it with. When I replied that I had literally been telling everyone she just shook her head, sadly. I was, it turned out, far too chatty to be a spy!

I've since been a music teacher, a social worker, a therapist, a blogger and now I'm a writer.

Life happens, plans shift and change and that's okay because people aren't trees – we aren't rooted to the spot, we can shift and change too.

did you know?

The average person has twelve different jobs during their lifetime.

You probably won't have just one career, and this gives you all sorts of interesting avenues to explore. Don't feel you have to know now what you will do in the long term – you just need a plan that's right for now.

the science bit

Your *prefrontal cortex* (the thinking part of your brain) is still maturing during your teen years so you might find planning and decision-making quite tricky on occasion!

when the destination is clear

If your plan is to be a dancer, you will know that you have to take many classes, be super fit and get lots of experience before auditioning for shows.

If you know where you are heading you can plot how to get there and confidently stride out in that direction.

when the destination is unclear

If your future plans are vague, that's fine too. Try and gather a range of useful skills and qualifications so when you do figure it out you will already have a lot of what you need.

It can help to spend time on career websites, talk to lots of adults about their jobs and get some voluntary experience behind you.

Motivation and inspiration are everywhere.

Reflect on your interests and skills too. The best careers combine making you feel engaged and energised with making use of your strengths and talents.

imagine your future

Get comfy and close your eyes. Have a little daydream about your life 10 years from now. See yourself smiling and happy, confident as you work and go about your life.

What are you doing?

Pay attention to what floats into your mind – you might find inspiration there.

create your own confidence...

...by giving yourself time to think or dream about the future you want (and remember, it is YOUR future – no one else's!).

11 fear busting

The act of doing something undoes the fear.

Shonda Rhimes, writer

Fears that stem from childhood can be embarrassing in your teens. Wanting to hold someone's hand in the park because you are scared of dogs is fine at 6 but at 16 may make you blush! Fears can interfere with life too – you might avoid camping with your friends because fear of the dark makes it feel impossible, or you'd love to go to a theme park with your friends, but you're terrified of rollercoasters.

what is fear?

Fear is simply an emotional reaction to something that feels unsafe. It is designed to protect us. The brain reacts to fear by sending signals to the body suggesting we run or fight (often referred to as 'fight or flight'). This causes us to tense up, feel stressed and stop thinking clearly. Fear feels horrible, and whether it's real or imaginary, your brain will respond to both in the same way.

imaginary fears

Imaginary fears might come from a story you have been told or a fear someone has passed on. Maybe when you were 5 your sister said she saw a ghost and ever since you've feared the dark.

It's hard to be logical when your emotional brain takes over, which is why you should plan to deal with fear when you are thinking clearly.

taking action

Imagine you are scared of drowning because you can't swim. By learning to swim you could undo that fear and increase your confidence around water. Confidence doesn't need to come first, you just have to take action.

exposure

Gradually getting used to the thing you are scared of makes facing it less overwhelming. This is called *exposure therapy* and it's a great way to build confidence.

Let's use this to tackle ***fear of the dark:***

First, make a list of your fear situations around being in the dark and rank them from least scary to most scary. Here are some suggestions:

- going to the bathroom at night without the landing light on
- sleeping with the bedroom door open so there is some light from the hall
- sleeping with the bedroom door closed and in full darkness
- sleeping at someone else's house with the door closed in full darkness
- going camping with friends with just a torch.

Next, make a list of what can help you face you fears. I call this a 'coping kit'. You might include:

deep breathing

music to distract you

support from a friend

yoga to relax you

a positive affirmation such as 'I can handle this'

Getting yourself into a relaxed state, having support, a positive mindset and distractions are all useful ways of coping.

Now that you have your plan and your coping kit, all you have to do is start.

Beginning with the least scary of your fear situations, the idea is to work on each one in turn until you feel ready to take on the next one. Every single action you take to expose yourself to your fear will help your fear shrink and your confidence grow, and doing it step-by-step makes it easier.

Why not try to tackle your fear this way on the next page?

what is your fear?

list situations you find terrifying from least (1) to most scary (5)

1 _____

2 _____

3 _____

4 _____

5 _____

my coping kit

_____

_____

_____

_____

_____

learning from others

Everyone has their own fears, and hearing about how other people have faced theirs can give you ideas about how to face your own. Ask three people you know to tell you how they overcame a fear, and you will be inspired.

be confident be you...

...by confronting your fears.

12 motivation

Today is your opportunity to build the tomorrow you want.
Ken Poirot, author and entrepreneur

It can be hard to feel motivated sometimes...

- to keep studying if you just want to hang out with friends
- to keep practising football if you never make the team.

There may be times when you start to think 'why bother?' But once you find your reason it is easy to reset your path.

two steps to success

The first step in finding your motivation is to ask **why** something matters. The second is to look at what you **can do** about it.

There are a number of things in life you can't control (like having to go to school and not getting in the team) but there are way more things you **can** control.

When you place your focus on what you can control, your motivation and your confidence get a fabulous boost.

Let's re-look at the areas above in light of this two-step approach.

football

Step 1: Think about **why** you want to be on the team.

Perhaps you love playing footie, enjoy team games and want to be super fit?

Step 2: Think about what you **CAN do** to meet those needs (outside of being on the team) and make a plan. You could:

1 keep practising (great for fitness)

2 try out for a different team/club

3 get your mates together for a weekly game at the park.

studying

Step 1: Think about **why** you need to study.

Perhaps it's because you want to get good grades, do a degree one day or get a particular job?

Step 2: Think about what you **CAN do** to keep studying, but also see your friends. You could:

1 create a timetable scheduling in time to both study and see friends

2 study with a buddy

3 reward yourself for studying hard with friend-filled Saturdays.

It is much easier to be motivated if you are super clear about your **WHY** and plan around what you **CAN** do (rather than bemoan what you can't). This approach will skyrocket your motivation and fill you with confidence because you will feel in control and empowered, and will want to succeed.

the science bit

Teens often get called lazy but actually the drop in *dopamine* (the happy hormone) during teenage years can really hamper motivation. Exercise gets your dopamine levels up  and makes you more productive, so getting up and getting moving is a great way to motivate yourself.

Rewards are highly motivating too. Research shows that rewards are responsible for three quarters of why people do things. So, when you have done some studying, THEN call your friend. Reward yourself for jobs well done.

find your motivation

Think about an area where you lack motivation and try the two-step approach. Focus on your WHY and list your CAN do, then try putting your plan into action.

What will you choose?

be confident be you...

...by focusing on what you **CAN do** and **WHY** it matters.

confident actions

:)

do you ever think to yourself?

If I was confident, then I would be braver.

If I was confident, I'd be more assertive.

If I was confident, I'd be able to speak in public.

You might assume confidence needs to come first, before you do something tricky, but it is in taking action that your confidence grows. Confidence doesn't need to come first; it is built on experience and accomplishment.

In order to act, most of the time you just need a good plan and some positive strategies, which is what this chapter has in store for you.

dent

Of course, you will need to take these actions in order to become more confident and that's down to you. But it is easier than you might think once you have a step-by-step guide to tackling the things you struggle with.

The consequence of walking a more confident path feels so good that you will be motivated to keep going. Remember, 'a journey of a thousand miles begins with a single step'.

It's now time to take positive action and to step into your confidence.

IONS

13 body confidence

> Wanting to be someone else is a waste of the person you are.
> **Marilyn Monroe, actress**

A mental health foundation survey discovered that 37% of teenagers have felt upset or ashamed of their body and worry about it daily. That needs to change.

If this affects you, here are ten steps to body confidence.

① be media literate

If you use social media, you will probably be bombarded with images depicting 'perfect' bodies. A lot of what you see on social media is advertising, encouraging you to buy something so you will 'look better'. Be conscious that a lot of this content is fake or contrived, and many of the images have been digitally altered.

Researchers have found that the more media-savvy teens are, the more body confident they are.

Try following social media accounts that celebrate body confidence rather than just body appearance, and you will see all bodies celebrated and yourself represented.

2 be curious

Think about why you look like you. Do you resemble other people in your culture or community? Perhaps you look like your cousins?

How you look is about far more than being 'attractive' – it's interesting, intriguing and part of your life story. Take pride in that.

3 focus on what your body can do

Do you have eyes that see, ears that hear and hands that hold? Your body is incredible and it can do so much. Give your attention to that rather than worrying about what it looks like.

4 be amazed

Did you know...?

- human teeth are just as strong as sharks' teeth
- your nose can recognise a trillion different scents
- you can see around one million colours

You have to admire your body, it's astonishing!

5 exercise

Exercise makes your body strong and toned and releases happiness-boosting endorphins. Exercise also gives you a glow (though that could be sweat!).

6 eat well

Eating healthily is an easy way to nurture your body and provide it with the fuel it needs. It also makes your teeth, hair and skin look better and boosts your body confidence.

7 experiment

If you aren't happy with your appearance, try experimenting. Change your hairstyle and try on a variety of clothes to find a style you like. Have fun with how you look.

8 be complimentary

If you heard someone tell your friend that they were too skinny or spotty, you would be appalled. Talking to yourself that way destroys your confidence. Instead, compliment yourself on your twinkly eyes, lovely curves or perfect stubble. It makes a huge difference.

9 embrace your uniqueness

Imagine if we all looked the same – how boring! You are a glorious individual, one in 7.8 billion. Embrace your differences, they are what make you special.

10 take care of you

Keep your hair conditioned and take care of your skin. Sleep. Use deodorant. Keep your teeth sparkly and your breath fresh. Take time to take care of yourself so you feel your best.

be confident be you...

...by enjoying, respecting, admiring and looking after your precious body.

14 avoidance

> You cannot find peace by avoiding life.
> **Virginia Woolf, author**

When you are struggling with your confidence, avoiding things may seem the best option. Avoidance means you don't have to do that tough homework, stand up to your friends, feel that grief, or ask out the person you have a crush on.

It means you:

- won't have to struggle
- can't get rejected
- won't get things wrong.

It may feel like a good way to keep yourself safe and be easier than doing what feels difficult, risky or uncomfortable.

It might make sense to your worried, stressed-out mind but avoidance can actually cause you BIG PROBLEMS.

the problem with avoidance

When you avoid doing what you want or need to, you may have averted something tricky (in the short term) but it won't bring you peace. Instead, you will just worry about getting behind or missing out, or the consequences of not dealing with something you should.

As well as bringing its own worries, avoiding issues can increase your problems in the long-run because...

What you resist, persists. Problems don't just magically disappear.

Imagine you have a toothache, but you hate going to the dentist. If you put it off your toothache will probably just get worse and worse until it becomes hugely painful. By the time you have no choice but to go, that small toothache has become a huge problem and you now need a lot of treatment.

Avoidance usually isn't worth it.

avoidance and confidence

Often, people avoid things because they lack the confidence to face them. But confidence comes from experience.

You may get rejected sometimes and, occasionally, standing up to someone won't go well, but you will learn from that. You will learn (from having a go) that you can survive things being imperfect and that it's not the end of the world if your attempts aren't 100% successful.

Often the things you face will work out and make life better, richer and more exciting. Don't wait until you feel confident before you stop avoiding things – instead, stop avoiding things and watch your confidence grow.

the science bit

A 10-year study of over a thousand people showed that those who used avoidance coping strategies had increased rates of depression and experienced more stress. Avoidance does not solve problems or build resilience, in fact it does the opposite: it makes us feel helpless and less confident.

So, the tough stuff? It needs to be faced.

avoiding avoidance

Think about this past week and all the things you have avoided. Perhaps you have avoided joining a new group, making a phone call, standing up for yourself or asking for help. Make a list of these things and over the next week try to get them ticked off your list. Do the easiest ones first and ask for help or support if you need it.

With each tick, your confidence will get a little boost and you will be motivated to try the next.

be confident be you...

...by being aware of the things you avoid and facing them instead.

15 volunteering

> As you grow older, you will discover that you have two hands – one for helping yourself, the other for helping others.
>
> **Audrey Hepburn, actress and humanitarian**

Volunteering makes a huge difference to the project you are supporting, whether you're helping at a foodbank or reading to someone who is lonely. The impact of your time and effort is priceless. And when you volunteer, you reap the benefits too.

how you benefit from volunteering

new skills

You will learn new skills through volunteering which is a great way to boost your confidence.

greater empathy

Volunteering can help you understand the challenges faced by others and help you become kinder and wiser.

increased independence

Doing something on your own, away from your home/school/friends is character-building and confidence boosting.

new relationships

It's a great way to meet people who share your values and visions and to make new friends.

work experience

Volunteering is great for your CV; prospective employers like to know that you know how to work.

pride and purpose

Volunteering adds meaning to your life – the positive impact you make will remind you that you matter and that your life has purpose. It is easy to be proud of yourself when you are helping others.

Just give it a go and you will feel instantly good about yourself.

the science bit

Volunteering is also a brilliant way to boost health. Studies have found that people who volunteer live longer than those that don't and they spend a lot less time in hospital! Volunteering also lessens pain and reduces the risk of heart disease. It is hard to be stressed when you are focused on other people or projects, and scientists believe this is one of the reasons it is so good for you.

get inspired

I have volunteered as a bingo caller, a reading helper, a summer camp counsellor, a pond clearer and a brownie guide leader and I could go on! This array of experiences was great fun and made me unafraid to try new things and meet new people.

Get inspired by asking the adults in your life about their volunteering experiences.

Lise's story

Lise works in Oxfam's charity bookshop on a Saturday. She helps organise the shelves and sell the books. She has made friends of all ages through her job, spends hours with her beloved books and has built up some brilliant work experience.

where to volunteer

Do-it.org is a database of UK volunteering opportunities. You can search by interest, activity or location and then apply online. You can also ask around; approach projects and charities directly or even create your own!

give volunteering a go

You could volunteer by shopping for a neighbour, mentoring a younger child at school, helping at an animal shelter... or any one of a million ways.

How are you going to put your compassion into action?

If you are unsure of what you could do, try listing the skills you already have and the things you enjoy doing, or think about the people around you and the sort of help they might need, and take it from there.

Start small but do start, the benefits are HUGE.

be confident be you...

...by making a difference.

16 goals

Having a goal with no plan of action is like wanting to travel to a new destination without having a map.
Steve Maraboli, author and motivational speaker

Reaching for a goal is like taking a journey, and every journey requires you to:

1 know where you are heading

2 plan your route

3 take what you need with you

4 start moving!

These are the same four steps you need to take when you set out to achieve your goals.

know where you are heading

You need to know where you are going before you can ever devise a route – therefore your destination (your goal) needs to be clear. It also needs to be realistic and achievable, or you will end up disappointed.

plan your route

Step by step is how you get from where you are to where you want to be. Divide your goal into smaller steps and celebrate as you achieve each one. This will motivate you to continue and feel confident about doing so.

be aware of obstacles

No matter how realistic your goal and how good your plan, LIFE can get in the way.

Stay focused on your goal, finding ways around obstacles or adjusting your route. Prepare to be flexible.

take what you need with you

What you take with you on your journey towards your goal matters. Try packing enthusiasm, hard work, resilience, dedication and a few cheerleaders too.

imagine arriving

Neurologists studying goal-setting found that brains cannot distinguish between reality and imagined reality. So, when you visualise achieving your goal, your mind starts believing it's real. It then drives you to take action that aligns with that belief, making success more likely. So visualise your goal succeeding – it's a powerful daydream!

start moving

Don't wait until you feel confident before you start to take action. Once you have all you need in place, simply taking steps towards your goal will bring you all the confidence you need. Just start moving!

Zander's story

Zander's goal was to become a lawyer. He had a plan:

1 Work hard at school.

2 Do well in his exams.

3 Go to university.

4 Become a lawyer.

It was a realistic goal but during his last year at school Zander's band started getting lots of opportunities and his studying paid the price. He didn't quite get the grades he needed to go to university.

But Zander didn't give up.

He re-focused on his goal and looked for a new path. He found a law foundation course at a local college and set to work. He smashed it. A year later Zander started studying at one of the best universities in the country.

He kept his eye on the prize, took responsibility, adjusted his route and took action. He is now well on the way to achieving his goal.

Going for your goals is worth the effort – it helps you feel capable, resourceful and independent and gives your confidence a boost too. It is a skill for life.

your goal

Decide on a goal you would like to achieve, either big or small. Follow the four steps described above, making a step-by-step plan, gathering the resources and support you need and then take ACTION!

Adjust your course if you need to, but don't forget to celebrate each step and watch your self-esteem bloom.

be confident be you...

...by going for your goals.

17 dealing with feelings

When awareness is brought to an emotion. power is brought to your life.
Tara Meyer-Robson. life coach

Ever wonder why your emotions feel so overwhelming and out of control? Well, it's all to do with your teenage brain.

what's going on?

The *amygdala*, the emotional processor in your brain, is super sensitive in your teens so you feel things strongly. Your *prefrontal cortex*, the area responsible for controlling emotions, isn't yet fully developed, which explains why you often act impulsively rather than thinking things through.

Life as a teen can be stressful with exam pressure, romantic relationships, body changes, arguments at home, and so on. No wonder some days your emotions feel overwhelming. However, there are things you can do to help you feel more in control.

taking control

Learning to calm down, process your feelings and manage conflict makes a difference to how confident you feel when dealing with your emotions.

Let's look at anger and the different consequences of reacting or responding:

Imagine that your little sister comes into your room, and you feel furious. You want privacy and have told her already to stay out. You get hot and bothered and shout at her. Your mum rushes upstairs, tells you off and confiscates your phone. Your sister cries. You're still angry and now you're in trouble too!

what you could do instead...

Instead, you go to the bathroom, splash cold water on your wrists to cool down and take deep breaths to slow your heartbeat. When you are calmer you can think more clearly.

You realise you are angry because you want privacy. You chat with your mum; explain how you feel and ask for a lock for your door. She agrees, impressed with your emotional maturity.

A thoughtful response always leads to better consequences than an impulsive reaction.

It's easy to make better choices when you...

pause and cool down

name your feeling

think through your options

respond

make better choices

- If you get a message that hurts your feelings, don't react by sending something spiteful back. Pause, cool down, consider your options then respond. Perhaps say 'Hey, that hurt my feelings' and see what the sender has to say.

- If your boyfriend is flirting with someone else and you feel jealous and insecure, rather than storming over and confronting him, pause, cool down and think through your options. You might want to ask a friend if they think it looks like flirting too?

Taking time to think before you act is always a good idea.

the science bit

Noticing and naming emotions jump starts the thinking brain, which enables the emotional limbic brain to calm down. That's why therapists say 'name it to tame it' when it comes to feelings.

calm-down lucky dip

Create a calm-down lucky dip by writing activities that calm you down on slips of paper and popping them in a bag.

Dip in when you need to for a chill-out prompt. It'll give you something new to focus on when you need to pause, and a fun way to calm down when you need it.

be confident be you...

...by dealing with your feelings in a positive way.

18 creativity

> The world always seems brighter when you've just made something that wasn't there before.
> **Neil Gaiman, author**

Do you remember as a child making mud kitchens, daisy chains and splatter paintings without any concern about how these would look or be judged? That carefree approach often changes as you grow up. In fact, studies show that 98% of 5-year-olds test as highly creative, yet only 2% of adults do.

Secondary schools tend to encourage correct answers over imagination. And in your teen years pressure to conform, together with self-consciousness, can also block your creativity. That's a shame because the benefits of creativity are varied and powerful.

the science bit

Studies have found that people who practise creative activities are happier and less anxious than those who don't. So, if you are feeling down or a bit stressed, being creative is a brilliant way to keep yourself mentally healthy and feeling good.

flow with it

Creativity often leads to *flow*. Flow is when you become totally absorbed in an activity like playing guitar, pottery, sewing or writing. Flow has been proven to boost a sense of wellbeing and of course it also provides a healthy mini-detox from technology.

Flow enables you to be mindful and completely in the moment. You can't worry about the past and future when you are absorbed creatively, and this gives your busy brain a rest.

time well spent

Being creative might look like you are just taking it easy. However, you could easily argue that you are working on your confidence and self-esteem because being creative can make you feel:

- accomplished
- skilful
- proud
- content
- relaxed
- rested

It is definitely time well spent.

divergent thinking

Creative thinking (also known as *divergent thinking*) is when you can see lots of different solutions to a problem.

There is no single right answer when you are being creative, so each time you are, you strengthen your divergent thinking skills and become a better problem-solver. It is a really useful life skill.

People who can solve problems well have more confidence in themselves as they trust they can cope with unexpected or tricky situations.

So yes, creativity is brilliant. It is good for your wellbeing, your confidence and your problem-solving skills and most importantly of all, it is fun. Hang on to it in your teens and it will serve you well.

confident creative you

Have a go at these creative ideas. Whatever creates more flow for you or makes you smile the most might be the one to pursue. Cross them off as you give them a try.

Sketch your pet

Learn to juggle

Invent a rap

Write your biography

Create a meal from the first five things you see in your fridge

Learn a dance

Make a happiness playlist

Create your name in nature with twigs, leaves and flowers

Photograph your family members in black-and-white profiles

Create something to wear like a scrunchie or a tie-dye t-shirt

be confident be you...

...by being creative.

19 how to say no

Saying no can be the ultimate self-care.
Claudia Black, actress

NO is a small but powerful word. It can protect you from all sorts of unhealthy and difficult situations, from skipping school to taking drugs. It can stop you from agreeing to do things you know aren't right for you.

In your teens, as you become more independent, your ability to make decisions in your own best interest becomes increasingly important. Being able to say no to things you don't want will help you stay true to yourself.

Sometimes it can be hard to say no, especially as a teenager, as it can be easier to go along with what other people are doing than to move away from the crowd and do the things that you want to.

blocks to saying no

You may worry that saying no will cause a confrontation or make you unpopular, or that you will get dumped or excluded.

Saying no can feel awkward, uncomfortable and risky. You might say yes just to avoid these feelings.

Wanting to please others at the expense of your own peace of mind is never okay. If YOU don't put your wishes first, who will?

the science bit

Research shows that people often choose what makes them happier in that moment rather than what will make them happier in the future, and that this can lead to reckless and damaging decisions.

When you wonder whether or not to say yes, think about tomorrow and the decision you will wish you had made.

confidence and saying no

The more you say no (and realise the world doesn't end as a result), the more confident you will be in saying it. Don't wait until you are confident to say no – say no first and your confidence will flourish.

the 'saying no' plan

You know what you should be saying no to in theory, but doing it in practice is often harder. Here are some things that could help:

1 Buy time

When you react quickly or emotionally, there is a risk that your decisions may be faulty. Try saying 'I'll call you back' or 'I'll let you know'. Use the extra time to get your thinking brain working or to talk over your no with someone you trust.

2 Suggest an alternative

If you want to refuse to do something but don't want to lose face, try suggesting something different. If friends ask to hang out the night before an exam, explain you have to study but will have them round to celebrate afterwards.

3 Blame your adults

Your teen friends might not like it but will understand if you say you just aren't allowed, or your parents say you have to be home – they will have rules too.

④ Gather support

Think about which friends share your values and back each other up or lean on each other when saying no feels lonely.

⑤ Have some stock phrases

Use 'No thanks, it's not for me' or 'Sorry, I can't help you with that' or simply just say 'No' – you don't have to explain.

⑥ Be clear

If you must, say no on repeat until it's heard. If this doesn't work then sometimes it is better to just physically leave the situation. It's not okay for people to try to talk you into things that you have already said no to.

the no list

Make a list of five things you want to say no to. Rehearse each situation using the strategies above.

Preparation helps when it comes to saying no.

be confident be you...

...by saying no when you need to.

20 marginal gains

> Most of the significant things in life aren't stand-alone events, but rather the sum of all the moments when we chose to do things 1 per cent better or 1 per cent worse.
>
> **James Clear, author and speaker**

Marginal gains are tiny improvements that, added together and over time, make a big difference.

let me tell you a story

In almost 100 years the British cycling team had only won one gold medal at the Olympics.

Apparently, they were considered so rubbish that one of the top European bike manufacturers refused to sell them bikes because they thought it would damage their sales!

But in 2003 everything changed.

Dave Brailsford became performance director of British Cycling. He introduced the concept of *marginal gains* to the team, based on the belief that if the team made 1% improvements in many different areas their results overall would improve dramatically.

So they improved the massage gel they used, they began wearing heated shorts, the weight of the tyres was adjusted, special pillows were purchased, they even had advice on how to avoid catching colds. In total, hundreds of 1% improvements were made and the results were amazing.

In the London 2012 Olympics the Team GB Cycling Team won a record eight gold medals!

why marginal gains work

Marginal gains offer manageable ways for you to confidently improve your life without you having to make huge changes that might feel overwhelming or stressful.

Growth mindset is a belief that abilities are never fixed and that you can always grow and improve. Making marginal gains is growth mindset in action.

A healthy, happy life is the result of lots of small decisions that lead you in a more positive direction, which in turn boosts your confidence. Can you find 1% ways to improve areas of your life?

little steps to big improvements

Think about how today has gone for you and write it up in bullet points, noting any tricky areas. Then decide on five small things you could change (marginal gains) to make your days better in the future.

Here's an example:

- Woke up at 7 a.m., left for school at 7.45 a.m. – as always, stressed and rushing.

> **Marginal gain: Set your alarm for 10 minutes earlier to reduce morning stress.**

- At lunch, spent ages queuing for food again – not enough time to hang out with friends.

> **Marginal gain: Make packed lunch the night before to avoid time spent queuing.**

- After school I scrolled on my phone until dinner then went swimming. Still doing homework at 10 pm and late going to bed.

Marginal gain: Do homework straight after school then reward your efforts with a little scrolling.

- Forgot one of my trainers for PE – oops!

Marginal gain: Keep PE bag fully packed, check and place it by the door ready for the morning.

- Got bus home from school, noisy and packed – arrived home feeling irritated.

Marginal gain: Walk home instead – fresh air and exercise after school is relaxing.

Keep up with your marginal gains all week and then reflect on how your days have been. I think you will be surprised how these small changes have made a big difference to you when added together.

be confident be you...

...by making tiny, consistent changes to improve your life.

21 make a bucket list

> If you want your life to be a magnificent story, then begin by realising that you are the author and every day you have the opportunity to write a new page.
>
> **Mark Houlahan, author**

A *bucket list* is a list of experiences or achievements you want to have in your lifetime before you 'kick the bucket'. You can call it a life-list if you prefer!

I made my first list aged 15 with my best friend. To our delight and astonishment, we have since achieved lots of the items on our lists including both of us writing books.

hope

Having goals and dreams for the future brings hope that life will be full, interesting, meaningful and exciting.

Your list should contain your dreams. You don't need to play it small or safe. It is a list by you and for you, so other people's expectations don't need to come into it. Let your imagination run wild.

variety

Some of the things on your bucket list may be small and fairly easy to achieve like *learn to juggle*; others might require saving up and planning such as *go on a safari*. Some might sit on your list for years before you achieve them.

Aim for a variety of goals; some life changing, some educational, some just for fun.

did you know?

The top ideas most often included in buckets lists are seeing the Northern Lights, swimming in each major ocean, becoming a millionaire, starting your own business, skydiving and having a family.

Making your own list will motivate and inspire you to try different things.

bucket list ideas

- Visit Egypt
- Ride a unicycle
- Raise £1,000 for charity
- Have a YES day

- Fall in love
- Learn to speak Italian
- Publish a poem
- Run a marathon

What could go on yours?

adding to your list

When you achieve your bucket list items it is immensely satisfying to cross them off your list. You might add to your bucket list throughout your life or alter it in some way and that's fine because the list is just for you.

When I was 49, I made a new list of fifty things to do before I was 50. I achieved forty of the challenges, which included giving a TED talk and getting a diploma in Tai Chi!

A bucket list helps you face the future with confidence, believing (knowing) that it is going to be full of adventures that you are going to make happen.

begin your bucket list

Grab a notebook and begin your bucket list. Can you think of ten things to add? Leave space after each one to write down how and when you achieved it. Is there anything on your list you could start working towards now?

If you wrote *learn to juggle*, maybe you could buy some balls and watch a video for beginners?

Your path to an exciting life has just begun.

be confident be you...

...by making your life a magnificent story.

22 asking for help

Ask for help, not because you are weak, but because you want to remain strong.
Les Brown, motivational speaker

Do you avoid asking for help out of fear that people will be annoyed, think badly of you or possibly say no?

It might help you to know that, according to research, your fears are largely unfounded.

If someone came to ask you for help, would you be annoyed or think badly of them? I bet you'd help them if you were able and, if not, you certainly wouldn't think any worse of them for asking.

did you know?

A Swiss study on helpful behaviour found that people who pledged to spend even a small amount of money on someone else rated themselves as feeling happier than those planning to spend it only on themselves.

It makes people feel good to help others. According to another study in the US, people who asked strangers for support received help at a rate that was 48% higher than they expected it to be.

So, ask with confidence. Most people will enjoy helping you and are more than willing to help if you ask.

a step in the right direction

When I was a student counsellor my students often began their sessions telling me they were at their 'rock bottom'.

I always explained that simply by asking for help they had actually left rock bottom and started the climb up. Asking for help is a step in a better direction because it starts to put you back in control.

Don't wait until you feel confident to seek out help, instead just do it and see your confidence grow as you reap the rewards.

when you need help to ask for help

If you feel nervous about asking for help, consider this:

1 The people you ask for help probably care about you and want things to go well for you.

2 If it's a professional you are asking then it is their job to help you and they will have chosen their profession because they enjoy helping people.

3 Asking for help stops you getting stuck, whether it's filling in a form for a job or mending a puncture on your bike. Problems need sorting; sometimes you can work it out yourself and sometimes you need help – the important thing is to get the problem fixed quickly so you can keep moving forward.

4 Small issues can become bigger if you don't address them quickly. Asking for support when you first need it is much better than waiting till you are overwhelmed, behind with your studies or becoming unwell.

5 Asking for help not only brings good advice but can also stop you feeling alone, which helps a lot when you are struggling.

list your helpers

Identify the potential helpers in each of these areas
of your life:

- Mental health
- Physical health
- Studying
- Friendship
- Personal relationships
- Career planning
- Identity
- Family problems

Add any other areas you can think of. Note them down
so you can turn to this list when you need help.

If you don't have cousins, friends, aunts, parents, teachers,
coaches, etc who fulfil these roles, look online for
organisations that can help or ask your GP or teacher to
direct you to the right people.

If you feel nervous about asking for help, you could just
send an email asking for what you need, but do always
reach out. Take that first step.

be confident be you...

...by always asking for the help you need.

23 say 'yes' to life

> Yes is a tiny word that can do big things. Say it often.
>
> Eric Schmidt, businessman

Saying YES to opportunities can be difficult when you are having a confidence wobble.

But, when you say yes to things, life becomes bigger, brighter and full of adventure, and the more experiences you have the more confident you will feel.

Let me tell you about GG.

Great Grandma (GG)

Great grandma (GG) was 75 when she moved from the village she had lived in all her life to be nearer her family. She missed her village but was determined to build a great new life.

In order to do this, GG decided to say yes to everything. If a neighbour said, 'Pop in one day for a cup of tea', GG was there next morning with her biscuits. If a leaflet came through the door about a new group or asking for volunteers, she signed up immediately.

By throwing herself into everything GG made new friends, developed new hobbies and had a full, meaningful life. She didn't stick with ALL the new friends and all the new hobbies but by saying YES to lots of things she was able to find ones she really liked.

Be more like GG (pop that on a sticky note to remind you).

if you don't say yes

If you don't say yes, you could miss out on all kinds of fun and opportunities that may not come around again... such as the school trip to France or the chance to try out for a theatre company.

There is a risk they might not work out (and you will cope if that happens) but unless you give them a go, the chances of them working out at all are absolutely zero.

the science bit

Shonda Rhimes is a writer and an introvert who researched what would happen if she spent a whole year saying yes to the things that scared her. In her book Year of Yes she concluded:

Anything that made me nervous, took me out of my comfort zone, I forced myself to say yes to. And a crazy thing happened: the very act of doing the thing that scared me undid the fear, made it not scary.

Enough practice and everything becomes easier.

start small

Your yes's do not have to be grand gestures, it's more about getting used to saying yes more often.

Begin by saying yes to:

- trying new food
- listening to new types of music
- reading books you wouldn't normally read.

Your aim is to get more comfortable with being uncomfortable (though you should never feel unsafe).

Taking your talent and skills, your *I can attitude* and your support team with you, begin to say YES to all aspects of life.

a yes a day

Think about a time when you said yes to something new and it worked out brilliantly.

Keep that thought in mind this week as you say yes to seven new experiences, big or small – one for each day.

Jot down how each one went and remember: it doesn't have to work out perfectly every time, it's all experience!

be confident be you...

...by saying yes to life more often..

24 problem-solving

Running away from a problem only increases the distance from the solution.
Anonymous

Are you a confident problem-solver or do you struggle when life gets tricky?

Problems can take many forms, from peer pressure to bullying and from French verbs to a fall out with a friend, but one thing is always the same – you can always do something to make things better.

Being a good problem-solver is not a fixed attribute. It is something you can work on through developing confident problem-solving skills and practising them.

avoid, dwell or explore?

If you *avoid* a problem it rarely goes away. It tends to just sit there, waiting, and sometimes it gets worse.

If all you do is *dwell* on your problem, turning it over in your mind and talking about it at length, it will just get bigger and bigger until it feels like a massive obstacle blocking your way. You will feel overwhelmed and full of worry.

If you move from dwelling on your problem to *exploring* it from different angles, you will start to feel more in control. You will begin to realise that you have options and you will start to see your problem as a challenge to overcome rather than as a roadblock.

Problem-solving happens when you face your problems and explore the many ways in which you could tackle them, and whilst this action-driven approach means you have to do some work and face what's wrong, it is the KEY to making things better.

A good way to solve problems is by using the STEP approach:

State the problem, as clearly as possible

Think about the different ways you could tackle it

Explore each option and think about its pros and cons

Pick one solution and give it a go

That's it. Simple. Problem-solving is not rocket science, it's just about following the four steps above no matter what the issue.

an example of the STEP approach in action

If your issue is that you have skin problems, addressing it with the STEP approach might look like this:

1 **State the problem** – I have acne, it's getting me down.

2 **Think about ways to tackle it:**

- See a doctor.

- Ask a pharmacist.

- Ask Jake (cousin) what he used to clear up his.

- Ask Mum to help me choose products to try.

3 **Explore each option** – all of these are good ideas, but it can take time to see the doctor and I'm way too embarrassed to ask Jake.

4 **Pick one solution** – I'm going to ask Mum to come with me to see the pharmacist, who can help us choose some products.

If this doesn't work, I'll then book an appointment to see the doctor.

Choices are clearer and less overwhelming when you take a step-by-step approach. As you develop your problem-solving skillset you will find your confidence in your ability to face and overcome challenges grows.

the science bit

Because your thinking brain is still under development in your teens, you might rely more on your emotional brain to make choices. Consequently, your response to problems might be emotional and impulsive. Thinking through solutions is always going to serve you better though, and a logical process like STEP will engage your thinking brain and help you focus. So remember: when faced with a problem, rather than react rashly, instead PAUSE then STEP.

STEP through your problems

Think of a small problem you have and try working through it using the STEP approach (you can always ask someone to help you while you get the hang of it).

be confident be you...

...by tackling your problems with a cool and confident mind.

25 body language

Few realise how loud their expressions really are
Richelle E. Goodrich, author

Think about a confident person you know – visualise them moving, gesturing and laughing. What do they look like?

They probably look relaxed, smile broadly, take up space with their body, laugh easily and focus on the person they are talking to.

Now think of someone who lacks confidence – are they folding their arms, speaking quietly, looking down and fidgeting?

Bodies speak a language of their own and communicate without saying a word.

the science bit

Scientists have discovered that 55% of communication is by body language, 38% by tone of voice and 7% by spoken words.

You may worry about the words you speak but actually your body and tone communicate more!

NVC

NVC is shorthand for *non-verbal communication*. It includes pitch, tone and volume of voice, gestures, expressions, posture, eye movement and contact, dress and appearance. It is very powerful.

NVC can:

- strengthen the message you're making verbally (a hug gives impact to a friendly hello)

- contradict the message you are giving (your voice might say, 'That's fine' but your tone may say, 'It's not!')

- act as a substitute for a verbal message (your red face can tell your parents they are embarrassing you without you uttering a word).

line things up

I once met with the guy who had burgled my home! He apologised for robbing me but didn't look in my direction. He was slumped in his chair with his feet up and tapping his pencil like he was bored. He might have been sincere but that wasn't the message I received so I didn't believe him.

For people to believe what you say, your body language and words need to match.

If you are annoyed and roll your eyes and scowl, everyone will hear you loud and clear. And if you want to exude confidence yet you're looking down, your confidence won't be heard.

change your body to change your mind

A study from San Francisco University, found that when you slump your body it's usually because you feel fed up or tired, but by sitting up straight you can improve your energy in an instant.

Brains take cues from bodies in just the same way that bodies take cues from our brains.

So, smiling makes you feel happier and standing with your feet apart makes you feel more secure. Try it. Use confident body language to make you feel more confident. It's not about faking it; it's about using it to change how confident you feel.

power posing

Social psychologist Amy Cuddy believes that *power posing* – standing in a posture of confidence, even when you don't feel that way – can boost your feelings of confidence. Her TED talk 'Your body language may shape who you are' has had 21 million views! Watch it yourself to find out more and learn some great power poses like this one:

The Wonder Woman pose

Stand with your feet apart, chin lifted and your hands on your hips.

Try holding the pose for two minutes then check how you feel. Are you feeling more confident than you were before?

be confident be you...

...by using your body language wisely.

26 resilience

Our greatest glory is not in never falling, but in rising every time we fall.
Confucius, ancient philosopher

Being resilient means being able to 'bounce back' when something challenging happens. It means being able to adapt and keep going when difficulties arise, rather than becoming overwhelmed.

The teen years are full of new challenges, and feeling strong and capable will help you cope with them.

the science bit

Research studies have found that teens who show high levels of resilience have fewer mental health problems. They also do better academically as resilience has been shown to have more impact than talent and intelligence when it comes to getting good grades.

Resilience is well worth working on.

how to boost your resilience:

remember how strong you are

Reflect on what skills and strengths you used in the past to get through difficulties, and what strategies helped. Perhaps your parents separated or you moved away from your friends?

How did you cope?

Looking at evidence of your past resilience will boost your confidence in facing any current or future issues.

increase your self-respect and self-compassion

If you are kind to yourself when things go wrong, you won't feel so low. And if you like yourself it is much easier to forgive your mistakes and move forward.

widen your social connections

Being part of different social groups (including outside of school) gives you more scope if one area of your life isn't going well and brings more sources of support.

develop your positive thinking

Focusing on what you **can do**, rather than what you **can't**, will help you to feel more in control. This prompts you to take action to make things better rather than simply feeling helpless.

take care of yourself

It's easy to let good sleep, healthy eating and exercise slip when times are hard but that will just make you feel worse. It's obvious but true: you need to take care of yourself before you can take care of anything or anyone else.

eat mindfully

process your feelings

Don't ignore how upset you are and just keep pushing forward. Instead, feel your feelings and listen to what they are telling you. Then move forward with a clear, calm mind to make good choices about your next step.

never walk alone

You never have to be resilient alone – professionals, family and friends will all be there if you need them. Lucy Hone, an expert on the subject, believes that supportive relationships are the most important factor in resilience, and we should create and nurture them.

People are not born resilient; they become resilient by practising the above skills. Try them and watch your confidence soar. You will begin to see you can cope, that you are strong and capable, and that you can always depend on... YOU.

hurting or helping?

Think of something you are finding hard and ask yourself this key question:

Is the way I am behaving in relation to this hurting or helping me?

If it is not helping you, think about what you can do differently. Jot down some ideas and take positive action.

be confident be you...

...by building up your resilience.

27 public speaking

90 per cent of how well the talk will go is determined before the speaker steps on the platform.
Somers White, management consultant

Like it or not there are times when you need to speak in public. Perhaps you'll need to present an idea in class, take a spoken language exam or even act on a stage?

If public speaking makes you anxious you might find you avoid these situations, or that they go awry because your nerves get the better of you.

the science bit

Fear affects both the mind and body.

The *amygdala* (the emotion processor in the brain) picks up on fearful thoughts and prompts stress hormones like adrenaline to flood the body, putting it on high alert.

Your muscles tense and your heart races and you feel ready for 'fight or flight'. This makes it difficult to think clearly and that's why you might forget what you have to say and want to run away.

But don't worry, you can change this.

what helps

Confidence isn't something you either have or don't have. It is not fixed; it is simply the result of the thoughts you think and the actions you take. This is great news because it puts you firmly in control.

With positive thoughts and actions in place you will be able to deliver what you want to say with confidence.

thoughts

Thoughts affect feelings so if you are telling yourself 'I can't do this' you will feel anxious. Try shouting 'Delete!' at such thoughts and intentionally thinking helpful thoughts such as 'I know what I want to say', and 'I have practised this' instead.

Thoughts like these will make you feel more in control and will make your mind calmer.

You can also calm your thoughts by calming your body. Try:

Progressive muscle relaxation (PMR)

Simply tense then relax your muscles, one by one. This releases tension in your body, which eases stress. Start with your toes and work your way up. Don't forget your shoulders, where lots of tension is held.

Deep breathing

Calming your breath will calm your mind. Try breathing in through your nose for 4 seconds, hold for 4 then breathe out for 4 through pursed lips. Deep breathing gets more oxygen to your thinking brain and tells your nervous system to chill.

Always think positively and calm yourself down before speaking in public. A calm mind is clearer and more focused.

step by step

Even if you don't have a big speech to prepare for, it is a good idea to practise public speaking, so that you are ready for when you do.

Practice is key to doing anything well.

You could practise talking about a hobby or your thoughts on a current issue and work through these steps:

1 Practise by yourself.

2 Practise out loud.

3 Try filming yourself and watching it back.

4 Practise again in front of a friend or adult.

Keep practising until you feel ready for your final performance.

Can you remember how many times you practised writing before it became easy to do? Well, the same goes for public speaking. Keep practising and your confidence will be high.

and smile...

TED talk researchers have found that smiles and hand gestures are the keys to a talk being popular.

People clearly like their speakers to be friendly and enthusiastic, so keep that in mind!

speaking practice

Prepare a 5-minute speech on your favourite meal and try working through the action steps above.

be confident be you...

...by speaking up and being heard.

28 risky business

> Don't let the noise of others' opinions drown out your inner voice.
> **Steve Jobs, entrepreneur**

Taking risks is about pushing limits and testing abilities and in your teens this is something you are more likely to engage in as you explore your identity and your independence.

Some risks are brilliant. These might include abseiling, travelling on your own or joining a protest.

Some risks are dangerous. These might include drug-taking, alcohol misuse or dangerous dares. Such risks can cause you harm and lead to problems in the future that would make you look back with regret.

the science bit

Two significant things are happening in your teen brain that make you more likely to take risks.

Dopamine is the hormone and neurotransmitter in your brain that's responsible for feelings of pleasure. Scientists have discovered that dopamine levels fall during teen years, which explains why you crave excitement and are frequently bored by 'ordinary life'. A big dopamine hit feels so good it can cause you to be impulsive and ignore warning signs.

Also, the *prefrontal cortex* – the thinking part of your brain that handles impulse control – doesn't mature until your twenties, which means right now you are likely to make less sensible decisions. So how can you confidently navigate risk when all this is going on in your brain?

pause

Pausing gives your emotional (impulsive) brain the chance to calm down and your thinking brain the chance to catch up. Taking 5 minutes to remove yourself from an argument, a bet or a dare gives you a chance to think, is this worth it?

5 minutes is nothing, but it could be everything.

reflect

When you pause, use the time to reflect on how you will feel tomorrow if you do this today, reflect on what could go wrong and on your values, and whether or not this behaviour fits with them.

Have the confidence to make the right decision for you.

self-awareness

Be aware of what it is that triggers you to take negative risks. Peer-pressure can be very strong – are you being pressured by friends or desperately trying to fit in with them?

A friend of mine avoided drink/drug pressure in his teens by saying he had a hockey match at the weekend and needed to keep his body fresh. His friends accepted that. Good friends will accept that you make your own choices. It is your responsibility to keep yourself safe even if they don't.

confidence-boosting risks

You can chase thrills in safe ways through sport, new challenges, and experiences. Schemes like The Duke of Edinburgh's Award can be exhilarating. These will boost your confidence, give you that dopamine hit and at the same time help you grow and push your boundaries in a safe way.

strategies for avoiding risk

What risky behaviour do you want to say no to?

Come up with three scenarios and work out with a friend or adult strategies or phrases you could use to take yourself out of those situations.

Try role-playing them. Find words that you would feel comfortable saying.

Practising risk-avoiding responses will increase your confidence in using them when you're in a risky situation.

be confident be you...

...by knowing your boundaries and how to keep yourself safe.

29 self-care

To love oneself is the beginning of a lifelong romance.
Oscar Wilde, poet and playwright

Do you take good care of yourself?

I don't mean the 'eat all the chocolate, ignore your homework and binge watch a Netflix series' kind of self-care. I am talking about the deeper, more nourishing stuff.

If you aren't sure, try answering the following questions:

- Do you exercise so your body is healthy?
- Do you eat well so you have energy throughout the day?
- Do you rest enough so your brain doesn't get frazzled?
- Do you spend time with people who care about you?
- Do you ask for help when you need it?
- Do you take social media breaks?

If not, then perhaps these are areas to work on? You deserve the best and you can provide that for yourself in so many ways.

Self-care is not about treating yourself, it is about looking out for yourself. It is making sure that you feel supported, healthy, clear-minded, calm, strong and confident. It's about having your own back and treating yourself with the same kindness, respect, care and attention you would someone you love.

a word about self-harm

Self-harm is when people deliberately hurt themselves to cope with painful or strong emotions. It can include a range of behaviours that are dangerous and damaging, including drug-taking, disordered eating and cutting.

If this affects you or someone you care about, you can always contact a supportive charity such as ChildLine or the Samaritans anonymously by telephone or webchat. Alternatively, talk to your GP, teacher or adults straight away.

Asking for help is self-care and self-care is always the best response if you feel in any kind of despair.

Ask yourself what would you tell a friend to do – then do that. Be your own best friend.

taking care of yourself

Self-care looks different for everyone but in your teens it can be broadly split into the categories of health, emotions, social life, home life and studying. Have a look below at the kinds of things you might include when looking at how to increase your self-care.

They might not sound as much fun as pizza and a pamper, but they will all nurture you and help you live your best life.

health

- Put away phone an hour before bed.
- Eat three meals + no more than one bag of crisps a day.

emotions

- Write daily gratitude journal.
- Listen to calming app.

social life

- Begin volunteering at wildlife trust.
- Distance self from X, they're too controlling.

home life

- Declutter room so it's a more relaxing space.
- Try to stop arguing with sister.

studying

- Make a revision plan.
- Tell History teacher I need some help.

your self-care chart

Make your own chart using the headings above and add two things to each that would increase your self-care. Commit to giving them a go over the next few weeks then re-examine how you feel.

Self-care works and it is your best defence against stressful, unhappy times.

be confident be you...

...by taking beautiful care of yourself.

30 being a confident student

Discipline is just choosing between what you want now and what you want most.

Abraham Lincoln, former US president

If you feel anxious or overwhelmed with schoolwork, there are ways to help yourself feel more confident.

don't stress

A bit of stress can be motivating but too much stress can make you feel overwhelmed, and this does not help clear-thinking or confidence.

You produce *cortisol* (a stress hormone) more easily in your teens so it's important to do what you can to keep stress at bay.

Activities proven to combat stress include:

- listening to relaxing music
- regular exercise
- being in nature
- having a routine
- reading for pleasure
- yoga
- meditation.

It is worth finding out what works for you and including it in your daily life.

ask for help

Do ask for help if you are confused with your schoolwork. If you remain stuck on one section then the next section of work will probably be tricky too. Asking for help when you FIRST need it can save you much bigger problems later (like when you have exams!).

Smart friends, siblings, and adults can be a good source of help, but your teacher will definitely be the one with the right answers.

avoid avoidance

Not doing homework and not revising might meet your desire in the short-term to do something more exciting (or just less dull), but long-term it will lead you to feel panicky and possibly doing pretty badly.

Tackle what you need to do FIRST then reward yourself with something fun.

sleep well

Research shows that teens need about 9½ hours of sleep a night. This can be a problem if you don't feel sleepy till past 11 p.m. and you have to get up at 7 a.m.

Sleep deprivation leads to more cortisol production and increased stress.

Your body clock changes in your teens, so you will want to sleep and wake later but school start times don't change. You need to try and get those hours in.

Here's what can help:

- avoiding caffeine from 2 p.m. onwards
- not napping during the day
- getting daylight and exercise during the day
- getting to bed by 10 p.m.
- having a milky drink
- having a bedtime routine
- trying a warm bath
- reading or listening to music before sleeping
- avoiding screen time for an hour before bedtime.

Good sleep matters because it helps your brain process what you have learnt during the day and helps you be wide awake for learning the next day. (It also stops you feeling grumpy.)

time management

Leaving things to the last minute is always a bad idea.

As soon as you have exam dates or a homework hand-in date, start allocating your time.

You will immediately feel more in control.

A diary or calendar can be useful for booking in study slots. Sticking to your slots and ticking them off when done will be satisfying and motivational.

take the long view

Keep your eyes on the prize. Doing your best at school leads to more choices in the future.

decisions, decisions

Being a confident student is not just about grades. It's about knowing you are in control and can handle your workload, stress levels, your sleep and your time management. Being a confident student is all about making good decisions.

You've got this.

be confident be you...

...by taking a positive approach to studying.

31 self-talk

> **Be very careful what you say to yourself because someone very important is listening... YOU!**
> John Assaraf, behaviour expert

Tell anyone they are stupid, rubbish, lazy, ugly or annoying and you will make them feel terrible. You will also dent their confidence, especially if you do this repeatedly.

I am sure you would never talk to other people this way but what does your self-talk sound like?

Self-talk is the way you talk to yourself, your inner voice.

If you call yourself names and put yourself down with your self-talk you are bashing your own confidence.

Not helpful.

But happily, the opposite is also true.

If your self-talk says that you are strong, smart, capable and resilient you will boost your confidence and feel amazing.

You cannot choose what others say to you but you can ALWAYS choose how to speak to yourself, so choose to be kind, positive and encouraging.

the science bit

Psychologist Ethan Kross from the University of Michigan, studied the pronouns people use when they talked to themselves. He discovered that the most effective self-talk is the kind where you refer to yourself by name.

So, I might say (when wrestling with shortbread):

'C'mon Becky you are great at baking, let's do this.'

Kross found that using your own name makes a difference because you are addressing yourself as you would other people and everyone tends to be kinder to other people than they are to themselves. It feels weird at first but do give it a go.

Scientists have also found that what we say to ourselves affects our behaviour.

In a study from the Netherlands, scientists watched women with anorexia walk through doorways. Even when they had lots of room some of the women squeezed sideways believing they wouldn't fit – they had told themselves so often that they were large, their mind and body now believed it, even though it wasn't true.

Self-talk is powerful.

think about your qualities

It can be hard to if you're used to being hard on yourself, but the following activity should help...

1 Write the words 'Who Am I?' in the middle or at the top of a page. Then write down twenty great things about you as they come into your head. JUST WRITE. Don't scrub anything out or worry if it's right or wrong. We promise it will give you a push.

2 Create a collage that celebrates your identity. You might want to include hobbies, interests, strengths, personality traits, likes and dislikes, beliefs, values, hopes and fears, dreams and ambitions.

affirmations

Affirmations are a great way to start practising helpful self-talk. Affirmations are short positive statements that are meant to be frequently repeated in order to get you thinking positively.

They usually begin with 'I am' or 'I can' followed by a positive quality or behaviour.

By using your self-talk to focus on positive aspects of yourself, you will encourage and motivate yourself to move away from negativity. This can change the image you have of yourself into a confident one and help you see your best self.

positive self-talk

Take one of these confidence affirmations and try saying it to yourself five times each morning this week as you look in the mirror, whilst brushing your teeth. Then pick another.

Make this a month of intentionally positive self-talk and see how it boosts you.

If you don't feel these things right now but want to, try adding 'I choose to believe' at the beginning of each affirmation.

be confident be you...

...by talking to yourself well.

I am capable of amazing things.

I believe in myself

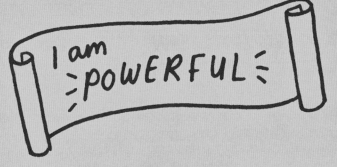

I am POWERFUL

I will do my best

I can do hard things

confident
relationships

:)

Everyone wants good Relationships that they feel confident about no matter who that relationship is with.

But being ⁑CONFIDENT⁑ in relationships might feel more challenging than having confident thoughts or taking confident action because one thing you can never ever control is other people. You can't control what people think of you or how they act towards you, and this makes relationships unpredictable.

What you can do though, in all relationships, is take care of yourself and stand up for yourself. Never be bullied or victimised, and if you are, get help fast. YOU matter most.

There is a lot you can do to strengthen how confident you feel in a relationship. You can learn to communicate clearly and assertively. You can learn to ease the pressure from

relationships that are stressing you out. And you can learn how to nurture and invest in the relationships that you want to flourish.

Being able to manage your relationships in a way that values and respects both you and others will give your confidence a boost.

Knowing how to create and maintain positive connections will also help you with situations where you are dealing with new people.

Let's take a look at how your relationships can be more positive and how you can feel more confident within and about them.

32 catching confidence

Surround yourself with people that reflect who you want to be and how you want to feel. Energies are contagious.
Rachel Wolchin, author

You may have noticed that when you are around happy people you smile more and are more enthusiastic. If the person you are with is feeling blue you probably find yourself smiling less and feeling pretty low too.

Feelings and behaviours can be caught, almost like a cold!

the science bit

The reason we pick up on people's feelings and behaviours is because we instinctively and unknowingly copy other people's body language and expressions.

Various studies have found that when we copy someone's expressions it causes reactions in our brains that lead us to feel similar emotions. This is called *emotional contagion.*

It is caused by mirror neurons in our brains that reflect what other people are feeling and enable us to feel the same emotion.

It's why you smile when a baby smiles (and feel happy) and yawn if someone yawns (and feel tired).

People who are sensitive pick up on other feelings and behaviours much more than those who lack sensitivity.

bad news

There are problems with emotional contagion. If you are scared, hanging around other people who are scared will only intensify your feelings as the other people's emotions affect yours.

And it works both ways.

If you are in a bad mood, other people around you might start being bad tempered too as your emotions affect them.

By being aware that you have caught or are spreading negative emotions, you do have the ability to walk away or to change the mood if you are getting others down.

good news

There are massive benefits to emotional contagion too that you can use to your advantage.

It can help you make wiser choices about who you spend your time with. To give your confidence the biggest boost you simply need to seek out joyful, confident people and spend more time around them.

That's it.

so, should you just ditch your unconfident pals?

Of course not.

They will have plenty to offer in the way of friendship even if they are not confident. But do be aware of how they affect your mood and your actions.

If all of your friends are too nervous to go to the school prom, for example, or try out for the school play, you could catch that anxiety and end up missing out too.

Keep an eye on that contagious low confidence and balance it out by spending more time with people who have a can-do, self-confident manner.

who gives you energy?

Write a list of the people you see on a regular basis.

Put a tick next to those people who give off happy, positive, confident vibes and who give you good energy when you see them.

These are the people who will help you feel more confident, and I would encourage you to spend more time with them.

be confident be you...

...by remembering that confidence is catching.

33 cheerleaders

Surround yourself with those who only lift you higher.
Oprah Winfrey, actress, author and entrepreneur

It is important to be able to rely on yourself when times are tough and to cheer yourself on when things are going well. But support from someone who has your back is a beautiful thing. And having a whole team of supportive people is even better!

The right people for your team will:

- listen
- encourage you
- help you find solutions
- gently push you to do better
- compliment you
- cheer you on
- believe in you.

They will also make you feel that you are good enough just by being you and that you matter, always.

the science bit

Research has shown that healthy, supportive relationships are brilliant for stress relief and improve both health and wellbeing. We feel so much more confident when our anxiety levels are low and we are feeling good!

Supportive relationships boost confidence and are worth investing in.

who makes the squad?

Don't restrict your team to only those of a certain age or gender. If you do, you'll be making your circle smaller than it need be. Think about the people in your life and how they support you:

- Does your grandma send you good-luck texts before every test?

- Does your friend get excited for you before a date and remind you how lovely you are if it doesn't go well?

- Does your swimming coach shout the loudest when you win and support the strongest if you lose?

Figure out who has your back and is rooting for you. These are the people you should share your dreams and your setbacks with. It doesn't matter if they are family, professionals, teachers, neighbours, coaches or friends, what matters is that you know who they are and you invest in these relationships.

If you don't have many supportive people in your life, seek new connections by saying YES to more opportunities and meeting more people. Then look out for people who seem warm and giving, and put your energy into building a relationship with them.

Warm people feel like sunshine.

giving back

When you know who you want on your team, you should nurture these relationships and make sure you give back.

Maybe your coach would like some cookies tied up with a label saying, 'Thanks for being great'?

All relationships, to be their best, need energy to flow both ways. So, cheer on those who cheer you on and give them a lift when they need it, just as they would do for you.

who DOESN'T make the team?

Over-competitive, over-critical, insensitive, jealous, disinterested folk need not apply! These people will do nothing for your confidence (except knock it) so treat these relationships lightly and don't make them more important than they are.

give thanks

We stand tall because of the people who lift us up and we should acknowledge them.

Get super comfy, play some relaxing music and one-by-one imagine your cheerleaders standing in front of you. Say a silent 'thank you' and give your heart a double pat before they leave.

When you have done this in your mind, might you try out that 'thank you' in person?

be confident be you...

...by recognising and nurturing your support team.

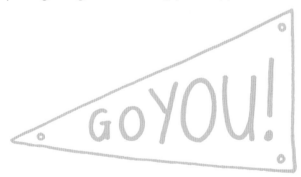

34 friendship

The only way to have a friend is to be one.

Ralph Waldo Emerson, preacher and poet

Researchers have found that people who had close friends in high school have higher self-worth and lower anxiety as adults when compared to those who might have been most popular but had more shallow friendships as teens!

Popularity isn't important but close friends are, so here are some great ways to up your friendship game.

think of friends like plants

Don't take old friendships for granted and just focus on shiny new ones. Friendships need to be treated like plants. They require a little sunshine, nurturing and attention in order to flourish. Neglect them and they just wither away.

appreciate differences

Friends do not necessarily have to look, think or behave like you. Be open-minded about who you are friends with. People who are different from you can be interesting, challenging and inspiring.

head for the warm people

Head for the people who feel like sunshine, those who are warm, open and welcoming. Being warm is so much more important than being cool. Be confident in your friendship groups and avoid ones where you are on edge or where you worry about fitting in.

manage your expectations

No single friend is going to meet all your friendship needs so don't expect them to. Some friends are funny, others are great listeners and some are practical. Appreciate them for what they offer rather than be disappointed in what they don't.

perfectionism

You aren't perfect and neither are your friends, they are human, and some days won't be their best. Don't write off a friendship for that. Be compassionate and empathetic and your friends will reflect that back when you aren't at your best. If you have any problems in your friendships, try to sort them out quickly and between yourselves – it makes life less dramatic and uncomfortable for everyone!

social media

Be careful what you say about your friends on social media – you might think you're talking in confidence to someone but a screen grab and a share take moments. A good rule to follow is if you wouldn't say something to someone's face, don't write it behind their back.

find your tribe

As you explore your identity and home in on your hobbies, you might feel it is time to make some new friends who are in tune with who you are now. Perhaps try a climbing school, an LGBTQ social group or a reading group to make like-minded friends. It's good to have someone by your side who shares your interests.

effort

You need to put your friendship into action through kindness, loyalty, time, effort, support, encouragement and reaching out both in good times and in bad.

reach out

Investing in your friendships pays off so today...

- contact a friend and compliment them
- contact another friend and encourage them
- contact a third friend and just ask them how they are.

be confident be you...

...by being the kind of friend you want to have.

35 *assertive* communication

The quality of your communication determines the size of your result.
Meir Ezra, business coach

Do people generally understand what you say, or does the meaning get lost or distorted somehow?

Perhaps you recognise your communication style from the list below?

being passive

Being *passive* in your communication means not expressing your wants and needs, mumbling 'okay' when you want to say 'no'. It means not raising your hand to ask questions and keeping quiet rather than sharing what's wrong.

Being passive avoids confrontation and the spotlight, but it never gets your needs met.

being aggressive

Being aggressive in your communication means you are loud and demanding. Perhaps you shout to be heard, slam doors, exaggerate or say unkind things.

Aggression may get you what you want but it won't earn you respect.

blaming/defending

Perhaps your communication style is making excuses, *blaming* other people or *defending* yourself?

This might get you off the hook but it never addresses the real issue.

being assertive

Assertive communication is where you convey what you want, need or think in a polite and confident manner.

here is how you do it:

- Speak in a clear and calm way.
- Use the word 'I' rather than 'You', which can come across as accusatory.
- State how you feel and what you would like to happen.
- Be accurate, don't exaggerate.
- Be factual.
- Repeat yourself if necessary.
- Be prepared to negotiate.
- Listen, then respond (rather than react).

assertive communication in action:

You: Hi Dad, hope you had a good day? I'm ready for a break. I want to go to Tia's for a few hours.

Dad: No, you're meant to be revising!

possible responses:

- 'Okay Dad.' – goes back to revising, feeling frustrated (passive).

- 'OMG you don't understand!' – shouts and slams door (aggressive).

- 'It's your fault I'm behind with revising, Dad, you didn't wake me up on time!' – stomps off (blaming).

Assertive response

You: I've already revised today. I want to go to Tia's then come back and continue. My teacher said it's a smart idea to have a break between subjects.

Dad: Okay then, that sounds good, have fun!

You won't get what you want every time you communicate assertively and clearly, but you have a much better chance – plus you will have kept your self-respect and shown respect to others too.

real life

Studies have shown that excessive social media use can interfere with communication skills as it reduces the experience of talking face-to-face and can make people feel awkward when they do.

So, try to get lots of experience of all types of communication: talking on the phone, not just texting, and using video calling (with people you know well). Perhaps pop over and chat with your gran or join your family at the dinner table and ask about everyone's day.

The more communication experiences you have, the better at it you will be and the more your confidence will grow.

practising assertiveness

Try asking for something you need from someone in your family using the guidelines above. Start small. If it doesn't work, try again with something else (people who refuse you a favour tend to be much more likely to agree if you ask them for a different one!).

be confident be you...

...by speaking clearly and assertively.

36 feeling socially awkward and self-conscious

> The reason we struggle with insecurity is because we compare our behind-the-scenes with everyone else's highlight reel.
> **Steven Furtick, pastor and author**

Do you ever feel self-conscious or socially awkward? Do you find yourself blushing, sweating, wanting to cry, not knowing what to say, or perhaps overwhelmed with embarrassment, wanting to be anywhere other than where you are?

Unfortunately, these uncomfortable emotions can be strong in your teen years and can really dent your confidence.

No matter how awkward or self-conscious you feel, it's important to remember that you're not the only one who feels that way and that there are things you can do to build up your confidence and make you more comfortable in social situations.

the science bit

Have you ever wondered why you are so self-conscious in your teens whereas when you were younger you would happily sing songs from *Frozen* to anyone who would listen, or run around doing dinosaur impressions?

It is partly because hormone changes at puberty have a huge effect on the brain, one of which is to flood it with oxytocin, the 'love hormone'. *Oxytocin* drives us to want to connect with others. This desire to bond makes us care deeply about how we appear to others, and that causes us to feel self-conscious.

Alongside this, researchers have found that being approved of by peers causes a big dopamine spike in teens, which feels amazing. This is why you can feel quite desperate to look cool in front of your peers.

Self-consciousness peaks around the age of 15. This explains why you might find your parents super-embarrassing at this time, especially if they treat you like a child in front of your friends.

what can help:

remembering it won't be forever

Understanding what happens to your brain through the teen years can help you to see that this isn't permanent or a character trait, but more an age and stage that will come to an end. Be assured that there is nothing about you which is wrong, and that your feelings are normal.

gathering support

Because this is a common experience you can find support, empathy and understanding from your friends and also from adults who really will have been through it too.

Try not to avoid situations and experiences because of how uncomfortable they make you feel. Instead, ask your friends to rehearse scenarios with you, help you prepare or, if necessary, tag along for moral support.

Do tell your adults what you need from them too – they can't mind-read and may have forgotten exactly how it felt to be a teen. Perhaps you could ask them to stop telling you to 'cheer up' or 'stop blushing', or teasing you in front of your peers. Explain to them that this simply makes you feel even more in the spotlight, which doesn't help.

refocusing

One of the best ways to ease the feeling of self-consciousness is to redirect your attention away from yourself and onto something or someone else instead.

Doing an activity as a group is easier than just hanging out socially. So rather than going to the park, try spending your social time at a dance class, conservation group. or ask if people want to go to the cinema. This might feel easier.

If you feel awkward in a social situation, shift the focus of attention onto someone else by asking questions and showing an interest in them. Let other people talk until you feel more comfortable.

food for thought

Despite any fears you may have, your teen peers are actually unlikely to be judging you at all – they are probably too busy worrying about how they appear themselves.

Try the activities on the next page. They will help you to stop focusing on how awkward you feel and instead think about how you can find connections with other people.

3-2-1

Think of **3** questions you could ask someone you have never met before, to help get the conversation going.

1 _____

_____

2 _____

_____

3 _____

_____

Think of **2** people you could talk to about feeling self-conscious, to help normalise the experience.

1 _____

_____

2 _____

_____

Think of **1** activity you could do with a group that would be so absorbing you would forget about how you appeared.

be confident be you...

...by not letting self-consciousness stop your fun.

37 word gifts

A compliment is verbal sunshine.
Atharva Veda, ancient Hindu scripture

When your confidence is high a compliment can be like the icing on the cake, an extra bit of 'feel good'.

Compliments (when you accept them) are just lovely – like tiny word gifts of motivation and encouragement that boost your confidence even further.

Compliments (when you don't accept them) can feel insincere and make you feel embarrassed and uncomfortable.

how good are you at taking a compliment?

Imagine you have recently performed in a school concert and your friend compliments you afterwards. Here are two possible conversations:

Friend: You sounded great in the concert!

You: No I didn't, I was awful. I got loads of notes wrong.

Friend: You were great.

You: No I wasn't. I made a mess of it. I'm so embarrassed, I should never have taken part.

(Now you both feel pretty rubbish.)

Let's try again...

Friend: You sounded great in the concert!

You: Aw thank you, that's so kind.

(Everyone feels great.)

Accepting a compliment with grace is a win for everyone; rejecting or minimising it makes everyone feel uncomfortable – so let's work on that.

the science bit

Researchers have found that praise activates the *striatum*, one of the reward areas in the brain, so accepting a compliment makes us feel just the same as if we had been given money.

Compliments are powerful!

But that's not all. Scientists have also found that when we are praised for a particular skill it can lead to an improvement in the learning that occurs during our sleep, a process referred to as *skill consolidation*.

So, compliments help you feel happier and perform better – both of which help your confidence rise.

keep those compliments

Every time you get a compliment that makes you smile, why not note it down in a journal to look back on when you need a boost?

Rather than deny or downgrade a compliment, simply smile and say thank you (nothing else is necessary) and then store it away for safekeeping.

Even if you don't agree with the compliment initially, it can be useful to consider it and reflect that perhaps someone sees something in you that you have not yet seen. Be curious about the compliments you are given. There's a very good chance you are more fabulous than you realise.

And don't forget – if you do something great, look particularly lovely or behave beautifully in some way, give yourself a compliment and note that down too.

be a giver

One great way to get more comfortable with compliments is to give more away. Seeing how good they make others feel will make you feel good too.

compliment yourself

If you had to give yourself a compliment right now, what would you say? Choose a compliment for each of the following:

- a talent you have
- an aspect of your personality
- the kind of friend you are
- something lovely about you.

Why not jot them down how good you feel about yourself right now?

_____

_____

_____

_____

_____

be confident be you...

...by accepting and enjoying the compliments you are given.

38 getting on with your adults

Adolescence is a period of rapid changes. Between the ages of 12 and 17, for example, a parent ages as much as 20 years.

Al Bernstein, sports writer and broadcaster

(Share this quote with your adults. I'm sure they'll agree!)

However confusing and emotional you find your teen years, you can pretty much guarantee that the adults in your life feel the same.

Just like you, they may feel sad that you seem to argue more now and don't feel as close. In fact they probably struggle to understand you just as much as you struggle to understand them.

times are changing

Everything changes for you in your teens. You are more attached to your friends, you make more of your own decisions, you explore your own interests and want increasing independence. All those things impact your family too and can feel scary for them.

You aren't ever responsible for how someone else feels but it is always good to be aware and to be sensitive towards other people – that's just part of caring for each other and having empathy.

empathy

Empathy is the ability to understand how someone else may feel. Empathy in action looks like this:

- If you go out, you keep your phone charged so they can contact you and vice versa.

- If you are going to be home late, you let them know so they can relax.

- If you are struggling with school, you tell them so they can support you.

- If you are upset and need space, you let them know that you're sad but okay, so they don't imagine worse.

The more you act with empathy, the more freedom your adults will give you as they trust you to make smart decisions. Behaving with empathy will also alleviate a lot of arguments.

If your relationship with your adults hasn't been going well, try to increase your empathy and make some effort to reconnect with them. This way, their confidence in you will grow.

the science bit

Adults may feel like the enemy sometimes, but they don't want to be and what you hear as anger is often simply worry.

Misunderstandings in communication are sometimes due to your teenage brain development.

Studies have shown that during the teen years, it is the emotional brain, rather than the thinking brain, that is used to interpret expressions. This is why it can be easy for you to misinterpret facial cues, mistaking fear, surprise and worry for anger.

So, before you get defensive or angry, check out your understanding of what your adult is really trying to communicate. Just ask. You might be surprised.

reconnecting

Try the three activities below to reconnect with your adults:

 Ask them about their own teen years and how they got on with their family (it'll help them to see things from a teen perspective again!).

- Suggest something you could do together, like playing a board game or doing some baking – they will be amazed and delighted, and it will only take 30 minutes of your time.

- Spend time looking through old photos together, remembering times when you felt close and happy.

be confident be you...

... by using empathy to create better relationships.

39 under pressure

When you say 'YES' to others
make sure you aren't saying
'NO' to yourself.
Paulo Coelho, author

Pressure in your teens can take many forms.

- You could be under pressure from friends to skip school, take drugs, bully, smoke or lie to your parents.

- In a relationship you may feel pressure to do things you are not comfortable with or spend more time with someone than you want.

- Your parents may pressure you to revise more, do more chores and help your sibling.

Additional pressure could come from coaches, teachers, even from yourself!

Pressure can lead to stress, overwhelm and burnout. If you experience this, you aren't alone. In a poll asking tens of thousands of high school students how often they felt stressed, 45% said 'all the time', and many attributed that stress to relationships.

the science bit

Researchers have found that stress can affect health in a variety of ways, including:

- headaches
- irritability
- sleep issues
- nausea.

It can also lead to mental health issues. A Norwegian study of one thousand teens found that those who spent time around people who pressured them struggled with anxiety and low mood.

Pressure from relationships is bad news!

make good choices

One of the easiest ways to reduce pressure is to make clear choices about what you will and won't do. For instance:

- If your friends want you to go to the cinema but you have revision to do, don't feel you have to try to do both. Make a choice. It's okay to tell your friends you have to revise and, if they keep pressing you, it's okay to switch off your phone. You can organise something social with them after the exam.

- In a relationship where you're being pressured to be more intimate than you like, you could choose to end it. People close to you should respect your boundaries and someone who doesn't respect you doesn't deserve you.

- If your parents want you to help clean, revise and listen to your sister read, tell them you can only do one of those things, so which do they prefer? Remind them *nobody gives their best when stressed* (a rhyme worth remembering!).

By reducing the amount of pressure in your life you will feel more confident and in control. Being honest about what you can handle and what you want reduces tension, bad feeling and friction in all of your relationships.

Of course, it might occasionally disappoint others but that's okay because your responsibility is primarily to you and in respecting you, others need to respect your choices.

DETOX BOX

take a phone break

It's great to be able to connect so easily via a mobile phone but constantly being contactable can put you under pressure to respond to every interaction.

In a survey on teen stress, almost 50% said that social media made them feel bad about themselves. Give yourself permission to turn your phone off sometimes.

It's amazing how stress lifts with a digital detox, even a mini one. I challenge you to do it for a day!

be confident be you...

...by removing some pressure from your life.

40 kindness

Be nice to people...maybe it'll be unappreciated, unreciprocated, or ignored, but spread the love anyway. We rise by lifting others.
Germany Kent, broadcaster

Kindness involves being gentle, caring, helpful, thoughtful, considerate and nurturing. It is the key to having good relationships with ourselves, other people and with the planet.

It makes the world a better place and, perhaps surprisingly, it can also help you feel more confident.

When you realise that the actions you take can make a difference, it not only makes you feel more confident, it can also encourage you to do more things to change the world in the future. Even the smallest action can have big consequences.

kindness and self-worth

Feeling confident begins with liking who you are, not just feeling good about what you can do or how often you succeed. Living in line with your values brings a deeper confidence, a sense of self-worth that is not easily shaken or quickly forgotten.

Everyone feels awful when you are unkind, including you. But when you are kind, it always feels good.

kindness is a strength

You might think that kindness sounds a bit flaky but it takes strength for people to be kind. It's what drives people to donate organs, offer time and money to charity, give blood, shelter refugees, become foster carers and rescue neglected animals. Kindness changes lives and sometimes it even saves lives.

kindness matters

Just notice how happy it makes others to receive your smile, your listening ear, your care, concern or attention. When you are kind, it is easy to see that you make a difference and that your actions have impact and meaning.

the (many) benefits of kindness

Being kind has been found to boost *serotonin* and *dopamine*, the neurotransmitters in the brain that give you feelings of satisfaction and wellbeing and which cause the pleasure and reward centre in your brain to light up. In fact, when you are kind to someone your brain experiences it in just the same way as if someone was kind to you.

Isn't that incredible?

Being kind has also been shown to lower *cortisol* (the stress hormone) and increase *oxytocin* (the love hormone), so you feel more relaxed and more connected to others.

Scientists have found that teens can even improve their mood just by thinking about a time when they were kind, and that kindness can help relieve both anxiety and depression.

It's fair to say that kindness has superpowers.

Have a go at some of these acts of kindness, and see your relationships blossom, your heart glow and your confidence soar.

Donate your pocket money to a children's charity

Take the school reception staff some cookies

Hold the door open for someone

Tell your best friend why you love them

Write yourself a letter of appreciation.

Help your sibling with their homework

Make a book box with a 'help yourself' sign and leave it outside your house

Help your parents around the house

Talk to the lonely kid at school

be confident be you...

...by spreading your kindness far and wide.

A JOURNEY
back to you

Throughout this book we have looked at how you can become more confident by taking care of your thoughts, your actions and your relationships in positive and proactive ways.

We have looked at managing how you view, present and think about your body. We have considered how you can speak up more clearly and assertively and even how you can speak confidently in public.

We've considered ways to boost your confidence in your creativity and in tackling fears, in facing your future and smashing your goals.

We've looked at how you can have better, less pressured relationships with people in your life and how you can be kinder and calmer and reduce the drama.

You now have a host of ways to boost your confidence and stride forwards into your life, no longer having to miss opportunities because you feel too nervous or too self-conscious to give them a go.

You have so many strengths and gifts to share with the world. You have beautiful relationships to form and brilliant opportunities to embrace. May you carry on with strength in the knowledge that you are amazing and good enough just as you are right now. And may you...

Go forth, be confident, be you.